Find Someone Who

Find Someone Who

Introducing 200 Favorite Picture Books

Nancy Polette

LIBRARIES
U N L I M I T E D
A Member of the Greenwood Publishing Group

Westport, Connecticut • London

Library of Congress Cataloging-in-Publication Data

Polette, Nancy.
    Find someone who: introducing 200 favorite picture books / Nancy Polette.
        p. cm.
    Includes index.
    ISBN 1–59158–465–5 (alk. paper)
    1. Picture books for children—Bibliography. 2. Children's literature—Bibliography.
3. Children—Books and reading. I. Title.
Z1037.P77 2006
011.62—dc22   2006027318

British Library Cataloguing in Publication Data is available.

Library of Congress Catalog Card Number: 2006027318
ISBN: 1–59158–465–5

First published in 2006

Libraries Unlimited, 88 Post Road West, Westport, CT 06881
A Member of the Greenwood Publishing Group, Inc.
www.lu.com

Printed in the United States of America

The paper used in this book complies with the
Permanent Paper Standard issued by the National
Information Standards Organization (Z39.48–1984).

10 9 8 7 6 5 4 3 2 1

CONTENTS

INTRODUCTION

Here is a fresh and fun approach to introducing 200 well loved picture books including many Caldecott winners and honor books.

Following a booktalk for each title for the librarian or teacher, children will discover what they have in common with the characters, settings, or plots of the stories when they are asked to find someone in the group or class who can claim ownership of one of the ten items given for each book.

The list can be read aloud to preschool children. For children who are reading, each child is given the list and circulates around the room to find someone who can claim one of the statements. A different person should be found for each statement.

For example:

For: *Hooway for Wodney Wat* by Helen Lester

FIND SOMEONE WHO . . .

1. Has been bothered by a bully _____

2. Has been a new student in a school _____

When the picture book is shared with the group, children will delight in seeing the similarities in their lives and the lives of beloved book characters.

ALADDIN AND THE WONDERFUL LAMP

by Andrew Lang; Illus. by Errol Le Cain, Viking, 1981

Aladdin, a lazy boy from a poor family, meets a stranger in the street who claims to be the boy's uncle. The man is really a wicked magician who forces Aladdin to go through a door underground and retrieve a magic lamp. By rubbing the lamp Aladdin releases a genie who sets him free. He uses the lamp to provide for his poor mother, to build himself a palace, and to win the hand of the princess. He and the princess are married but the evil magician returns and must be dealt with before Aladdin and his bride can have true happiness.

FIND SOMEONE WHO . . .

1. Would never speak to a stranger on the street _____

2. Can name a story with a lazy person _____

3. Has watched a magician perform _____

4. Has a basement in his or her home _____

5. Can name a story with a princess _____

6. Can draw a picture of a magic lamp _____

7. Can say two words that rhyme with LAMP _____

8. Has built a palace out of blocks _____

9. Has no brothers or sisters _____

10. Has given his or her mother a gift _____

THE ALPHABET TREE

by Leo Lionni, Knopf, 2004

Suppose you were very small and lived with others as tiny as you at the top of a tree. This is where the tiny alphabet letters lived. When a strong wind began to blow you can imagine what happened. All of the little letters were blown off of the leaves where they lived and found themselves on the ground at the bottom of the tree. If they were able to climb back to the top of the tree the same thing would happen when the next strong wind blew. Along comes a word bug who understands the problem of the little letters. Becoming strong is easy, the word bug told them. And he showed them how!

FIND SOMEONE WHO . . .

1. Has a tree in his or her yard

   _____

2. Can say the alphabet in order from A to Z

   _____

3. Can name one good use of wind

   _____

4. Has climbed a tree

   _____

5. Has jumped in a pile of leaves

   _____

6. Has held a bug in his or her hand

   _____

7. Can make four new words using the letters in ALPHABET

   _____

8. Knows a word that is the opposite of STRONG

   _____

9. Has had a hat blown off by the wind

   _____

10. Can say the last four letters of the alphabet backwards

    _____

ALWAYS ROOM FOR ONE MORE

by Sorche Nic Leodhas; Illus. by Nonny Hogrogian, Holt, 1965

Lachie was a very friendly fellow. He lived with his family in a small cottage. No matter how small the cottage, visitors were welcomed with open arms. Lachie invited a tinker, a tailor, a young lass, an old woman, a bagpiper, and many others to share the hospitality of his home. As more and more visitors arrive the cottage is filled with singing and dancing and with too many people. Finally the cottage collapses. To solve the problem Lachie builds a bigger house where there is always room for one more.

FIND SOMEONE WHO . . .

1. Likes to have a lot of company _____

2. Has a first name that begins with the letter L _____

3. Can name a friendly character in a book _____

4. Will sing a song for the group _____

5. Is taking dancing lessons _____

6. Knows what a bagpiper is _____

7. Knows what a tailor does _____

8. Has a sister who is a teenager _____

9. Has more than one grandmother _____

10. Has moved to a bigger house _____

AMAGING GRACE

by Mary Hoffman; Illus. by Caroline Binch, Dial, 1991

Grace was a little girl who loved the stories her grandmother told her. In fact, she loved them so much that she would act out all the parts. When her teacher announced that the class was to present Peter Pan as a play, Grace knew she would make a wonderful Peter Pan. Her classmates told her that she could not play the part because Peter Pan was a boy and he wasn't black. But when time for try-outs came, Grace was by far the best Peter Pan and after the evening performance she felt as if she could "fly all the way home." Her mother had told her all along that she could achieve anything she wanted if she tried hard enough ... even "fly all the way home!"

FIND SOMEONE WHO ...

1. Likes to listen to stories

_____

2. Has had a part in a play

_____

3. Likes to act out stories

_____

4. Has a grandparent living with them

_____

5. Has seen live dancers on a stage

_____

6. Has been told "You can do it if you try"

_____

7. Can name something you would find in New York City

_____

8. Has taken dancing lessons

_____

9. Likes to play dress up in fancy clothes

_____

10. Knows what a ballet is

_____

AMELIA AND ELEANOR GO FOR A RIDE

by Pam Munoz Ryan; Illus. by Brian Selznick,
Scholastic, 1999

It was a beautiful April evening in 1933 when Mrs. Roosevelt invited Amelia Earhart, her husband, George Putnam, and several other friends to dinner at the White House. Amelia mentioned how beautiful Washington, D.C. would look from the sky at night. She invited Eleanor to go for an airplane ride. Both ladies left the dinner party and, dressed in their long gowns, boarded a plane for a flight over the city. When they returned, Eleanor invited Amelia to see the city by land from her new sports car. Here is a true account of two adventurous women and one very special evening when they made dreams come true.

FIND SOMEONE WHO . . .

1. Knows who lives in the White House

   _____

2. Can name the wife of the United States president

   _____

3. Has flown in an airplane

   _____

4. Knows what chowder is

   _____

5. Has helped set the table for company

   _____

6. Knows what the job of a reporter is

   _____

7. Does not like to get dressed up

   _____

8. Likes angel food cake better than any other cake

   _____

9. Can name the capital of the United States

   _____

10. Has taken pictures with a camera

   _____

AMELIA BEDELIA GOES CAMPING

by Peggy Parish; Illus. by Lynn Sweat, Greenwillow, 1985

Amelia Bedelia is the Rogers family maid who takes everything literally and misunderstands homophones and homographs. "Hitting the road" means taking a stick and hitting the road to Amelia Bedelia. "Putting stakes in the ground" means getting steaks (meat) and burying them. The Rogers family hopes to sleep in the tent and asks Amelia Bedelia to pitch the tent. She finds it is too heavy to pitch and gets some boys to help her. They pitch it into the bushes. As you can see this is one camping trip the Rogers family won't soon forget.

FIND SOMEONE WHO . . .

1. Likes to go camping

    _____

2. Knows what a homonym is

    _____

3. Has ridden in a truck

    _____

4. Has spent a night in a tent

    _____

5. Has helped build a campfire

    _____

6. Has roasted marshmallows over
   a fire

    _____

7. Can name an animal you would
   find in the woods

    _____

8. Has gotten water from a well

    _____

9. Knows what a chigger is

    _____

10. Can name three things to take on
    a camping trip

    _____

AMOS AND BORIS

by William Steig, Scholastic, 1971

Amos is an adventurous mouse who builds a boat and takes it out to sea. Unexpected trouble comes and he is stranded in the middle of the immense ocean, a thousand miles from land. Luckily he meets a friendly whale named Boris who is willing to help Amos to get back home. What could Amos do to return the favor? Read this exciting book of great adventure and friendship to find out.

FIND SOMEONE WHO . . .

1. Knows what a hurricane is

2. Can name a story about a whale

3. Has told someone good-bye for the last time

4. Has built a toy boat

5. Has helped someone in trouble

6. Has fallen into a river or lake

7. Has taken home a stray animal

8. Has seen a real elephant

9. Knows the name of an ocean

10. Has caught a mouse and let it go

AND THE DISH RAN AWAY WITH THE SPOON

by Janet Stevens and Susan Stevens Crummel, Harcourt, 2001

Hey diddle diddle, the cat and the fiddle, the cow jumped over the moon. The little dog laughed to see such sport. Is something missing from this nursery rhyme? Yes! The last line is missing. The dish really did run away with the spoon and if they don't return the entire rhyme can't be read. To remedy the situation the dog, the cat, and the cow set off to find the dish and spoon. Along the way they find both friends and danger as they meet the spider that frightened Miss Muffet, the Big Bad Wolf, and Jack in the Beanstalk. After much searching they find the dish that is broken. What will they do now?

FIND SOMEONE WHO . . .

1. Knows someone who plays a fiddle

   _____

2. Has a dog for a pet

   _____

3. Has had a cat that ran away

   _____

4. Can say a nursery rhyme

   _____

5. Has broken a dish

   _____

6. Has searched for something that was lost

   _____

7. Is not afraid of spiders

   _____

8. Can tell you what Jack got when he traded the cow

   _____

9. Knows where Miss Muffet sits

   _____

10. Has helped to set a table

   _____

ANNIE AND THE WILD ANIMALS

by Jan Brett, Houghton Mifflin, 1985

It had been a long winter and the snow was falling. Annie could not find Taffy anywhere. Annie waited and waited but her cat did not return so Annie decided to make some corn cakes and leave them at the edge of the woods to attract another small animal to be her pet. She could not believe it when a moose, a wildcat, a bear, and a stag appeared. What will Annie do? Will she ever see Taffy again?

FIND SOMEONE WHO . . .

1. Has had unexpected company for dinner

   _____

2. Has a cat for a pet

   _____

3. Has had a pet that ran away

   _____

4. Can name a wild animal that lives in the woods

   _____

5. Likes cornbread

   _____

6. Has gone walking in the woods

   _____

7. Has seen a real bear

   _____

8. Can name a wild animal whose name begins with the letter M

   _____

9. Has a cat that has had kittens

   _____

10. Has a pet other than a cat

    _____

ARROW TO THE SUN

by Gerald McDermott, Viking, 1974

In this Native American folktale from the Southwest, the Lord of the Sun sends a spark of life to Earth and creates a boy. Because the boy has no father he is teased and then shunned by the other youths of the tribe. The boy's one goal in life is to find his father so he sets out on a journey. There is no help to be had from Corn Planter or Pot Maker but when the boy reaches Arrowmaker he is in luck. Arrowmaker turns the boy into an arrow and shoots him to the Sun who sets four difficult trials to be overcome before he will acknowledge the boy. The boy is successful in meeting each trial and finally in being claimed as a son by the Lord of the Sun.

FIND SOMEONE WHO . . .

1. Has finished a difficult job

2. Can name a Native American tribe

3. Can name a famous Native American

4. Has made something from clay

5. Has had a sunburn

6. Has shot an arrow from a bow

7. Can name a state located in the Southwest

8. Can make two other words using the letters in FATHER

9. Can say a word that rhymes with ARROW

10. Can tell in what direction the sun rises

AUNT HARRIET'S UNDERGROUND RAILROAD IN THE SKY

by Faith Ringgold, Crown Publishers, 1992

Harriet Tubman was a very brave woman. She was a slave who escaped to the North yet went back to the South many times; first to rescue family members and then to rescue many other slaves she did not know. The journey to freedom was called the Underground Railroad. Harriet led the escaped slaves from one place to another. Sometimes safe houses were found along the way where the escaped slaves could rest and eat. It was a difficult and dangerous journey yet Harriet made it many times. This dream story tells of this courageous woman and the Underground Railroad.

FIND SOMEONE WHO . . .

1. Knows what courageous means

2. Can explain the purpose of the Underground Railroad

3. Has a first name that begins with the letter H

4. Can take one letter from SLAVES to tell what Harriet Tubman did for many slaves

5. Has been on a long trip

6. Has ridden on a real train

7. Has a last name that begins with the letter T

8. Can name another brave person

9. Has had to do a difficult job

10. Can name another group of people who escaped to freedom

A BABY SISTER FOR FRANCES

by Russell Hoban; Illus. by Lillian Hoban, Harper & Row, 1964,
Reprinted in HarperCollins Treasury of Picture Book Classics, 2002

Frances has a new baby sister and she is feeling neglected. Mother doesn't have time to iron her blue dress for school or to shop for the raisins she likes on her oatmeal. No one seems to pay attention to her songs and rhymes so Frances decides to run away. She packs her blanket, her doll, her money, a box of prunes, and some cookies and chooses under the dining room table as the best place to run away to. In her run away place Frances hears her parents talk about how they miss her poems and songs and how a baby sister really needs a big sister. Frances decides to return home when she realizes that "a baby is not a family."

FIND SOMEONE WHO . . .

1. Has a baby sister   _____

2. Is named Frances   _____

3. Likes oatmeal for breakfast   _____

4. Can say a poem   _____

5. Likes to eat dried prunes   _____

6. Has a favorite hiding place   _____

7. Can sing a song for the group   _____

8. Has a blue dress or shirt   _____
9. Can tell of a time when he or she
   has helped a younger sister or
   brother   _____

10. Is the oldest child in a family   _____

11. Has a favorite blanket   _____

THE BEARS ON HEMLOCK MOUNTAIN

by Alice Dalgliesh; Illus. by Helen Sewell, Simon & Schuster, 1992

Jonathan lived in a stone farmhouse at the foot of Hemlock Mountain. Grown-ups did not think there were bears on the mountain but Jonathan did. Besides, Uncle James said he had once seen a bear. When Jonathan's mother sent him over the mountain to borrow a large cooking pot from his aunt, the boy is late in returning and a search party goes out looking for him. What they find is a surprise for everyone!

FIND SOMEONE WHO . . .

1. Has visited or lived on a farm

2. Has two grandmas and two grandpas

3. Has had more than 20 people for dinner

4. Can name three different animals that might live in the woods

5. Has climbed a mountain

6. Has done something to worry a parent

7. Can sing a favorite song

8. Has seen a real bear

9. Has played Hide-and-Seek

10. Has forgotten to do something he or she was asked to do

BEAUTY AND THE BEAST

Illus. by Warwick Hutton, Atheneum, 1975

A father is caught picking a flower for his daughter and must promise the owner beast to send his daughter to live in the beast's castle. The daughter goes willingly but at first fears the beast who really means her no harm. After a time the girl, Beauty, comes to see the beast's inner qualities of love and kindness. When the beast appears to be close to death, Beauty give the beast a kiss that transforms him back into his original princely shape.

FIND SOMEONE WHO . . .

1. Can name three fairy tales with a heroine

   _____

2. Has picked flowers from a garden without asking permission

   _____

3. Has received a gift from a father who has been away on a trip

   _____

4. Has a first name that begins with the letter B

   _____

5. Would rather be handsome or beautiful than rich

   _____

6. Would rather live in a castle than in a large house

   _____

7. Has two sisters

   _____

8. Likes the rose better than any other flower

   _____

9. Can name another tale with a beast

   _____

10. Can find a word in BEAST that gives a direction

    _____

BEDTIME FOR FRANCES

by Russell Hoban; Illus. by Garth Williams, HarperCollins, 1960

Frances, like many children, has problems at bedtime. She needs a glass of milk and many kisses before being tucked into bed with her teddy bear and doll but it is not yet time for sweet dreams. Up she pops to tell her parents that there is a tiger in her room, a giant in the corner, and a crack in the ceiling that is getting wider. But finally a different kind of bumping and thumping puts Frances to sleep.

FIND SOMEONE WHO . . .

1. Can name a scary noise _____

2. Likes peanut butter and crackers _____

3. Has an 8 o'clock bedtime. _____
4. Can name 3 different animals whose names begin with the letter B

   _____

5. Has stayed awake until midnight _____

6. Has seen a real tiger _____

7. Can name a story with a giant _____

8. Has seen a teddy bear _____
9. Can name a bedtime snack with a long A sound

   _____

10. Can name a bedtime snack with a long E sound

    _____

BERLIOZ THE BEAR

written and illustrated by Jan Brett, G.P. Putnam's Sons, 1991

Poor Berlioz the bear! On the day of the ball he has all kinds of trouble. First, there is a strange buzzing noise in his double bass. Next, the wheel of the wagon transporting the musicians gets stuck in a hole. How can they ever get to the ball on time? Just in case they do make it, the musicians put on their tail coats and tune up their instruments. Other animals who are passing by stop to help. In turn, a rooster, a cat, a billy goat, a plow horse, and an ox pull on the rope to get the mule to stand up. Nothing happens. The dancers are waiting in the town square. The clock chimes eight, time for the ball to begin. Berlioz is out of ideas. There seems no way to get to the ball until a buzzing bee helps out.

FIND SOMEONE WHO . . .

1. Has been stung by a bee _____

2. Has been late to a party _____

3. Has seen a live bear _____

4. Is learning to play an instrument _____

5. Has heard a rooster crow _____

6. Has a cat for a pet _____

7. Has a dog for a pet _____

8. Has ridden in a wagon _____

9. Knows what DESPERATION means _____

10. Likes to dance _____

THE BIG SNOW

by Elmer and Berta Hader, Macmillan, 1976

The days were getting colder. A flock of geese in their V formation was headed south, a sure sign that winter was coming. Little rabbit listened as his mother told him the days of winter were coming soon. A groundhog looked up and saw the geese. He knew it was time to begin his long winter nap. He would not awaken until early spring. All of the animals of the woods knew that when the snows came that food would be hard to find. A little old man and little old woman knew this, too. A rainbow around the moon told the owl that the expected snow would fall at any moment and it did. It was a big snow but the animals found food … it had been put out for them by the old man and woman.

FIND SOMEONE WHO . . .

1. Can name three things that tell winter is coming

   _____

2. Has caught a wild rabbit

   _____

3. Can describe the formation of flying geese

   _____

4. Knows in what month Groundhog Day comes

   _____

5. Has an older person as a friend

   _____

6. Has walked alone in the woods

   _____

7. Has made a snowman

   _____

8. Has a bird feeder at home for winter birds

   _____

9. Can name three colors in a rainbow

   _____

10. Can name the first day of spring

   _____

THE BIGGEST BEAR

by Lynd Ward, Houghton Mifflin, 1952

Everyone in Johnny Orchard's town had huge bearskins hanging on the sides of their barns. Everyone's, that is, except Johnny's barn. His barn didn't have one, and this was very humiliating for Johnny. He was determined to have a skin hanging on his barn as well, so Johnny went hunting for his own bear, the biggest bear. Johnny did come back with his bear, but it was far from big; in fact it was a little cub. But that little cub brought big trouble.

FIND SOMEONE WHO . . .

1. Has climbed an apple tree

2. Has seen a real bear

3. Has lived on a farm

4. Has a wild animal for a pet

5. Has played in a barn

6. Has walked alone in the woods

7. Has visited a zoo

8. Knows someone named Johnny

9. Has set a wild animal free in the woods

10. Can name three wild animals whose names begin with the letter B

BLUEBERRIES FOR SAL

by Robert McCloskey, Viking, 1976

A mother and her child go berry picking on Blueberry Hill. Mother wants to can the berries for winter. A mother bear and her cub go berry eating on Blueberry Hill at the same time. Mother Bear wants her cub to eat lots of berries to get ready for winter. Imagine the surprised mothers when they turn around to find each other's children behind them! Both mothers walked quickly away ... mother to find Sal and Mother Bear to find her cub. All ends happily when the mothers and children do find each other.

FIND SOMEONE WHO . . .

1. Has eaten something that contains blueberries

   _____

2. Has seen a real bear cub

   _____

3. Has picked some fruit with a parent

   _____

4. Has gotten lost from a parent

   _____

5. Knows someone named Sally

   _____

6. Has filled a basket with something

   _____

7. Can name two animals that begin with the letter B

   _____

8. Can name a word that rhymes with SAL

   _____

9. Likes to walk in the woods

   _____

10. Can name a word that rhymes with BEAR

   _____

BOXES FOR KATJE

by Candace Fleming, Illus. by Stacey Dressen-McQueen, Farrar, Straus & Giroux, 2003

After World War II there is little left in Katje's town of Olst in Holland. Katje's family must go without soap and milk and must patch and repair clothing. Then a mysterious box arrives from America. It was sent by Rosie, a little girl from Indiana, to help the people of Europe. Katje is delighted with the soap and the socks but most of all with the chocolate. She writes a thank you letter that begins an exchange of letters between the two girls and more boxes for Katje and the people of Olst so that the people stayed warm and well fed all through the cold winter.

FIND SOMEONE WHO . . .

1. Knows the year the United States entered World War II

   _____

2. Has written a letter to a stranger

   _____

3. Can name a city in Holland

   _____

4. Can name two things to eat made with chocolate

   _____

5. Can name the capital of Indiana

   _____

6. Would like to receive soap as a gift

   _____

7. Has received a gift from overseas

   _____

8. Has the first name of Rose or Rosie

   _____

9. Can name a town in the United States that begins with the letter O

   _____

10. Can name two countries in Europe

    _____

THE BOY OF THE THREE-YEAR NAP

by Dianne Snyder; Illus. by Allen Say, Houghton Mifflin, 1988

Taro, a Japanese youth, is the Boy of the Three-Year Nap. Taro is well known throughout the village as a lazy good-for-nothing. His widowed mother must work to put food on the table and Taro does nothing to help. The day comes when the lazy youth falls in love with the daughter of a rich merchant. Knowing that the merchant would never give his permission for his daughter to marry Taro, the youth devises a scheme to win her hand. He dresses up as a local god and tells the gullible merchant that his daughter must wed the laziest boy in town. Not only that but the merchant must rebuild Taro's mother's house. Taro is allowed to marry with the merchant providing all the money he needs.

FIND SOMEONE WHO . . .

1. Can find Japan on a map _____

2. Lives or has lived in a small town of village _____

3. Has a mother who works outside the home _____

4. Knows someone who takes a daily nap _____

5. Knows a woman who is a widow _____

6. Has been tricked by someone else _____

7. Has attended a wedding _____

8. Can make two different words using the letters in TARO _____

9. Has a father who has a daughter _____

10. Has worn a disguise _____

THE BREMEN TOWN MUSICIANS

retold by Ilse Plume, Doubleday, 1980

A very old donkey ran away from its master, taking the road to Bremen where he hoped to find a job as a musician. On the way he meets a dog and a rooster. They team up and find a cottage in the forest where they hear robbers plotting. With each animal on the other's back they stand tall and make such a noise that the robbers run away into the forest. With the robbers gone, the animals are happy to have a snug cottage for the night.

FIND SOMEONE WHO . . .

1. Can name four different farm animals

   _____

2. Has heard a rooster crow

   _____

3. Has a dog and a cat at home

   _____

4. Plays a musical instrument

   _____

5. Sings or has sung in a choir

   _____

6. Has spent a night in a small cottage

   _____

7. Has been frightened by noises in the night

   _____

8. Can name another story with animal characters

   _____

9. Knows the name of one famous musician

   _____

10. Can make four other words using the letters in TOWN

   _____

BRINGING THE RAIN TO KAPITI PLAIN

by Verna Aardema; Illus. by Beatriz Vidal, Dial, 1983

This is the great Kapiti Plain, all fresh and green from an African rain. But one year the rains were very late and a terrible drought descended. The beautiful plain grew barren and dry until Ki-Pat, watching his herd of hungry and thirsty cows, spied a cloud hovering above and came up with a way to green up the grass, all brown and dead, that needed the rain from the cloud overhead.

FIND SOMEONE WHO . . .

1. Knows if Africa is a country or a continent

   _____

2. Has experienced a time of drought

   _____

3. Has been hungry and thirsty

   _____

4. Likes to walk in the rain

   _____

5. Can say two words that rhyme with RAIN

   _____

6. Has watered flowers

   _____

7. Knows why the Earth needs rain

   _____

8. Had watched someone milk a cow

   _____

9. Likes milk better than any other drink

   _____

10. Has a first name that begins with the letter K

    _____

THE BUTTERFLY

by Patricia Polacco, Philomel, 2000

The time is World War II. Monique discovers a young Jewish girl and her family who have been hiding in the basement. They have to hide because they are Jewish, and the Nazi soldiers are looking for them. Knowing that she cannot go outside, Monique brings the little girl grass, flowers, and beautiful butterflies. On a night when the little girl comes to play with Monique in her room they are are discovered by a neighbor. Because of this, the Jewish family must flee. The escape is full of danger and Monique wonders if her friend has made it to a safe place. She is reassured when she sees many butterflies fly at her window … her friend, she believes, has found freedom like the butterfly.

FIND SOMEONE WHO . . .

1. Has a first name that begins with the letter M

2. Has a basement in his or her home

3. Has kept a secret for more than one month

4. Knows someone who fought in World War II

5. Can find France on a map

6. Can say "Hello" in French

7. Has caught a butterfly

8. Has given a favorite possession to a friend

9. Can name three different flowers

10. Can name another story where someone has to escape

CAPS FOR SALE

by Esphyr Slobodkina, Harper & Row, 1947, Reprinted in
HarperCollins Treasury of Picture Book Classics, 2002

There once was a peddler who had many caps for sale. He wore all of the caps on the top of his head. First he put on his checked cap, then all the caps were stacked on top of the checked cap: gray, brown, blue, and red caps. He walked through the village calling "Caps for sale," but no one wanted to buy a cap. The peddler was hungry and having no money to buy food he decided to take a walk through the country. Before long he went to sleep under a tree and when he awoke he found monkeys, high in the branches of the tree, were wearing his caps … all but the checked one. He pleaded for the return of his caps but the monkeys ignored him until he threw his checked cap on the ground and the monkeys did the same. The peddler returned to the village to sell his caps once more.

FIND SOMEONE WHO . . .

1. Knows what a peddler is   _____

2. Has taken a walk in the country   _____

3. Has tried to sell something no
   one wanted   _____

4. Has a red cap   _____

5. Has gone to sleep under a tree   _____

6. Can say a word that rhymes with
   CAP   _____

7. Wanted to buy something but had
   no money   _____

8. Knows where you can see a real
   monkey   _____

9. Has worn two caps at the same
   time   _____

10. Bought a new cap in the last
    week   _____

CHERRIES AND CHERRY PITS
by Vera B. Williams, Greenwillow, 1986

Bidemmi is a little girl who loves to draw. She lives in the city and her drawings are about the people she sees there. She begins with a dot, then draws a line and explains as she draws what her drawings are about. Each drawing has a person who takes red, ripe cherries home to others…a man to his children, a lady to her parrot, and a boy to his sister. When Bidemmi gets a bag of cherries of her own, she saves the pits and plants them, and with loving care, helps the cherry tree to grow so that she can share rich, ripe cherries with her neighbors.

FIND SOMEONE WHO . . .

1. Likes to draw pictures _____

2. Has lived or lives in a big city _____

3. Can name three foods made with cherries _____

4. Has a grandmother who likes to tell stories _____

5. Has lived or lives in an apartment _____

6. Has planted some seeds _____

7. Has watched something grow from seeds _____

8. Can name a word that rhymes with PITS _____

9. Has made something for another person _____

10. Can name a word that rhymes with CHERRY _____

CHESTER'S WAY

by Kevin Henkes, Greenwillow, 1988

Chester was a creature of habit. He had only one way to cut sandwiches, to get out of bed, to tie his shoes, and had the same thing for breakfast every morning. Chester's friend, Wilson, was happy to do things Chester's way. They dressed the same on Halloween, shared the same umbrella, and raked leaves together. Then Lilly, who had her own way of doing things, shows up. At first Chester is disturbed at having his routines interrupted. Then he begins to see that different does not mean wrong and that changing the way you do things can sometimes make life more fun.

FIND SOMEONE WHO . . .

1. Can name one thing he or she does the same way every day

   _____

2. Has dressed the same as a friend on Halloween

   _____

3. Has a first name that begins with the letter C

   _____

4. Has a first name that begins with the letter L

   _____

5. Makes his or her own sandwiches for lunch

   _____

6. Is wearing shoes that don't tie

   _____

7. Has a friend whose first name begins with the letter W

   _____

8. Has shared an umbrella with another person

   _____

9. Likes cereal best for breakfast

   _____

10. Likes to do things the same way every day

    _____

CHRYSANTHEMUM

by Kevin Henkes, Greenwillow, 1991

Because her parents thought she was an absolutely perfect baby they gave her a very special name, Chrysanthemum. Chrysanthemum loved her name especially when mother used it to wake her up or father used it to call her to dinner. But going to school for the first time was a shock. The other children made fun of her name. They said it was too long and would not fit on her name tag. They said she was a flower to be picked and smelled. Each day Chrysanthemum took longer and longer to get to school. When she was chosen to be a daisy in the school musical the children laughed again. But the music teacher saw nothing funny about being named for a flower because her name was Delphinium. When the girls heard this, they all wanted flower names as well. Chrysanthemum bloomed!

FIND SOMEONE WHO . . .

1. Is named after a flower _____

2. Likes to go to school _____

3. Has made fun of someone _____

4. Likes music class best _____

5. Likes art class best _____

6. Has a first name of more than 8 letters _____

7. Has been teased by someone else _____

8. Would never make fun of another person _____

9. Can name a word that rhymes with SCHOOL _____

10. Can name three different flowers _____

CLICK, CLACK, MOO COWS THAT TYPE

by Doreen Cronin; Illus. by Betsy Lewin, Simon & Schuster, 2000

Farmer Brown has a problem. His cows like to type. All day long he hears click, clack, click, clack, moo. But Farmer Brown's problems really begin when his cows start leaving him notes. They demand electric blankets because the barn is cold at night. Not only do they demand the blankets, but they refuse to give milk until they receive the blankets. Farmer Brown is furious and refuses to give the cows the blankets so the cows go on strike and will not give milk. The hens, who are cold, too, join in the strike and refuse to lay eggs. Duck serves as the neutral party and takes the notes back and forth between the farmer and the cows. When the cows offer to give up their typewriter in exchange for the blankets, Farmer Brown agrees and the farm gets back to normal operation... almost!

FIND SOMEONE WHO . . .

1. Has lived on or visited a farm _____

2. Likes milk better than any other drink _____

3. Has tried to milk a cow _____

4. Has gathered eggs from a hen _____

5. Has a typewriter at home _____

6. Has seen a duck in a pond _____

7. Knows someone who has gone on strike _____

8. Likes scrambled eggs for breakfast _____

9. Can sing a song about a farmer _____

10. Can say three words that rhyme with COW _____

CLOUDY WITH A CHANCE OF MEATBALLS

by Judi Barrett; Illus. by Ron Barrett, Atheneum, 1982

There were no supermarkets in the town of Chewandswallow since breakfast, lunch, and dinner fell from the sky. Breakfast began with a shower of orange juice followed by low clouds of sunny-side-up eggs and toast. Lunch might be frankfurters already in their rolls followed by mustard clouds. People listened to the weather report to find out what they would be eating the next day. It was quite a nice arrangement until one day the weather took a turn for the worst. The food that fell from the sky got larger and larger and so did the portions. The residents of Chewandswallow feared for their lives and had to escape. They floated on large slices of stale bread for a week until they reached a town that welcomed them. This is the tall tale Grandfather loves to tell.

FIND SOMEONE WHO . . .

1. Knows what a tall tale is _____

2. Can name two different grocery stores _____

3. Can tell you what a Sanitation Department does _____

4. Likes pancakes for breakfast _____

5. Can name one reason a town is abandoned _____

6. Can name four foods in a well balanced meal _____

7. Can name one food from the sky _____

8. Can name one food from the ocean _____

9. Can name one food from the land _____

10. Can name five fresh vegetables you can buy at the supermarket _____

THE CLOWN OF GOD

by *Tomie dePaola,* Harcourt, Brace, Jovanovich, 1978

Young Giovanni of Sorrento was known throughout Italy as the marvelous juggler with the clown face. As the years passed he became old and he and his talents grew feeble. He was forgotten by those who loved him. Taking refuge in a church on Christmas Eve, he watched the procession of the gifts in awe. After everyone had left, he offered the only gift he had to the image of the Christ Child: his juggling. It was then that the miracle occurred.

FIND SOMEONE WHO . . .

1. Has watched a clown at the circus   _____

2. Has an older person as a friend   _____

3. Has gone to church on Christmas Eve   _____

4. Has tried to juggle   _____

5. Has seen a real juggler perform   _____

6. Has been made up with a clown face   _____

7. Has given a gift to a stranger   _____

8. Can find Italy on a map   _____

9. Can make four words that end with OWN   _____

10. Can make four words using the letters in TALENTS   _____

CORDUROY

by Don Freeman, Viking, 1968

Corduroy was a small stuffed bear who sat on the toy shelf of a large department store. He wished more than anything for a child to take him home but it never happened. Then one day a little girl spotted him on the shelf and knew that Corduroy had to be her bear even though he was missing a button. That night Corduroy goes throughout the department store searching for his lost button. Finally he does retrieve the button and is found by the night watchman who puts him back where he belongs on the toy shelf. The next day the little girl returns and takes Corduroy home where he discovers what a real home is like.

FIND SOMEONE WHO . . .

1. Has lost a button _____

2. Has a teddy bear at home _____

3. Has shopped in a big department store _____

4. Has visited a toy store _____

5. Knows a girl named Lisa _____

6. Knows someone who is a night watchman _____

7. Has a relative who is a salesperson _____

8. Has a stuffed animal other than a bear _____

9. Can name three words that rhyme with BEAR _____

10. Has saved money to buy a toy _____

CRICTOR

by Tomi Ungerer, HarperCollins, 1958

Madame Bodot taught school in a small French town. Her son, who was in Africa, sent her a small snake that she named Crictor. Crictor went to class and made letters and numbers with his body. Children used him as a jump rope and to practice tying knots. Also he rescued their kites when they got stuck on high wires. One night a burglar broke into Madame's house but Crictor's quick thought and actions saved the day. The villagers rewarded the snake with a medal.

FIND SOMEONE WHO . . .

1. Can name a town or city in France

   _____

2. Can say "Hello" in French

   _____

3. Knows whether Africa is a country or a continent

   _____

4. Has held a snake in his or her hand

   _____

5. Can name a way to make letters without a pencil, pen, crayon, or marker

   _____

6. Can say a jump-rope rhyme

   _____

7. Has had a kite caught in wires or a tree

   _____

8. Knows what a burglar is

   _____

9. Has won or knows someone who has won a medal

   _____

10. Can add three numbers in his or her head

    _____

DANDELIONS

by Eve Bunting; Illus. by Greg Shed, Harcourt, 1995

Leaving the home that she knows to settle in a new and different land is not easy for Zoe's mother who is also expecting a baby. The family sets out from Illinois in an ox-drawn cart and takes the family cow with them. When they reach their destination on an almost barren plain with no neighbors in sight, Mama feels more and more discouraged. The family works together to dig the well and to build their house of sod. It looks so much like the rest of the plains that it is hard to see when they get only a short distance from it. After a trip to town Zoe brings back dandelions and plants them on the roof of the sod house, which gives a cheerful welcome to visitors and family alike.

FIND SOMEONE WHO . . .

1. Has moved to a new town or state _____

2. Has a new baby brother or sister _____

3. Has watched someone milk a cow _____

4. Knows what sod is _____

5. Has drunk water from a well _____

6. Has had a yard full of dandelions _____

7. Lives at least two miles from a town _____

8. Can spell ILLINOIS _____

9. Knows what a pioneer is _____

10. Can give the title of another book about a pioneer family _____

THE DAY JIMMY'S BOA ATE THE WASH

by Trinka Hakes Noble; Illus. by Steven Kellogg, Dial, 1980

Another boring day at school. Nothing exciting ever happens! Nothing unless you consider crying cows and pigs on a school bus exciting. Nothing exciting except maybe food fights with corn and eggs. Nothing exciting except spending the day with boa constrictors, pigs, sheep, chickens, and other assorted farm animals. I suppose it could be exciting, if you like that kind of stuff.

FIND SOMEONE WHO . . .

1. Has ridden on a school bus _____

2. Has lived on or visited a farm _____

3. Can name five different farm animals _____

4. Can name five foods grown on a farm _____

5. Has lost a pet _____

6. Has taken part in a food fight _____

7. Has helped someone do the wash _____

8. Has had a snake for a pet _____

9. Has gone on a class field trip _____

10. Can name five words that rhyme with SNAKE _____

DEAR MR. BLUEBERRY

by *Simon James,* Simon & Schuster, 1996

It is vacation time so Emily has to write to her teacher for help: "Dear Mr. Blueberry, I love whales very much and I think I saw one in my pond today. Please send me information about whales." Mr. Blueberry answers at once, pointing out that whales live in salt water, not in ponds so it can't be a whale. After several letters Mr. Blueberry explains more forcibly that a whale cannot live in Emily's pond. Emily then reports that her whale has become migratory and has left the pond. She is sad. But in her last letter she has a happy surprise to tell Mr. Blueberry and all is well.

FIND SOMEONE WHO . . .

1. Has written a letter to a teacher _____

2. Has seen a real whale _____

3. Can name a story that has a whale as a character _____

4. Has a wading pond in his or her yard _____

5. Likes cornflakes for breakfast _____

6. Knows what MIGRATORY means _____

7. Has gotten lost while out with a parent _____

8. Has traveled a long distance _____

9. Knows someone named Arthur _____

10. Can name three other ocean creatures _____

DIARY OF A WORM

by Doreen Cronin; Illus. by Harry Bliss, Joanna Cotler Books, 2003

Suppose a worm kept a diary. What do you suppose the worm would write? Here are the thoughts of a worm who wears a red baseball cap, goes to school, and has homework just like children. However, while children look forward to a fishing day, the worm digs deeper to stay out of sight. Worms don't have to worry about taking baths or going to the dentist but they do worry about being stepped on. Some tasks that are easy for children like making a macaroni necklace are a challenge for a worm but some tasks, like making a tunnel, are easier for a worm than for children. The worm's diary is complete with photos of his family.

FIND SOMEONE WHO . . .

1. Has fished using a worm for bait _____

2. Does homework before watching TV _____

3. Likes to go to the dentist _____

4. Has stepped on a bug _____

5. Likes to take a bath _____

6. Keeps a diary about daily activities _____

7. Has made a macaroni necklace _____

8. Has a red baseball cap _____

9. Has made a tunnel in the sand at the beach _____

10. Would like to have a worm for a pet _____

DINORELLA

by Pamela Duncan Edwards; Illus. by Henry Cole, Hyperion, 1997

Dinorella is dying to go to the dance, but her dreadful stepsisters, Dora and Doris, declare she's too dowdy and dull, so Dinorella is stuck in the den doing dishes. Then Fairydactyl arrives and bedecks Dinorella with some dazzling diamonds. Dinorella departs for the dance, but on the way witnesses a dastardly deed, involving the Duke and a disgraceful Deinonychus. Dinorella must carry out a daring plan to save the day but in the process looses her dazzling diamond. The Duke sets off to find the damsel who owns the jewel. Will he find Dinorella or will Dora or Doris become the Duke's bride?

FIND SOMEONE WHO . . .

1. Likes to listen to fairy tales
   _____

2. Knows what DOWDY means
   _____

3. Can say a sentence with each word beginning with the letter D
   _____

4. Can name three different dinosaurs
   _____

5. Has seen a real diamond
   _____

6. Has a first name beginning with the letter D
   _____

7. Has two sisters
   _____

8. Will perform a dance for the class
   _____

9. Knows what a domestic is
   _____

10. Can name an animal that lives in a den
    _____

THE DINOSAURS OF WATERHOUSE HAWKINS

by Barbara Kerley; Illus. by Brian Selznick, Scholastic, 2001

Benjamin Waterhouse Hawkins had a passion. Growing up in London in the 1800s he loved to draw and sculpt dinosaurs. As a young man he dreamed of creating life-sized dinosaurs and convinced Richard Owen, a scientist who studied the structure of bones, to help him. Queen Victoria was quite taken with the idea and provided the money so that Benjamin could create dinosaur statues. While creating the statues Benjamin invited many scientists to a New Year's Eve party that was held inside a monstrous model of an iguanodon. After building his statues for the Queen, Benjamin was unsuccessful in creating the statues in the United States but many still stand today where they were first built in Sydenham, England.

FIND SOMEONE WHO . . .

1. Has the first name Benjamin

2. Has a last name beginning with the letter H

3. Has traveled to England or who can find England on a map

4. Has made animals out of clay

5. Has made a soap sculpture

6. Can name the current Queen of England

7. Can name three different dinosaurs

8. Has attended or given a New Years Eve party

9. Can name a movie that features dinosaurs

10. Knows what ANATOMY means

DON'T LET THE PIGEON DRIVE THE BUS

by Mo Willems, Hyperion, 2003

Imagine how foolish these instructions sound from a bus driver who leaves the bus for a short time. Before leaving he says, "Don't let the pigeon drive the bus." Within a short time, along comes a pigeon. "Hey, can I drive the bus?" the pigeon asks nicely. When he is told NO, he tries again. "I tell you what: I'll just steer," and "I never get to do anything," then "No fair! I bet your mom would let me." Not able to convince anyone that he should be allowed to drive the bus, the pigeon goes wild and screams, "LET ME DRIVE THE BUS!!!" The driver returns, and the pigeon leaves still upset until he spies a huge tractor trailer that probably would be much more fun to drive than a bus.

FIND SOMEONE WHO . . .

1. Has seen a pigeon on a roof _____

2. Has taken a short ride on a bus _____

3. Has driven something with a motor _____

4. Knows a bus driver's name _____

5. Wanted to do something but was told "NO" _____

6. Has taken a long trip on a bus _____

7. Can make three new words with the letters in PIGEON _____

8. Can name two other means of public transportation _____

9. Can name three things to drive other than a car _____

10. Can name two birds smaller than a pigeon _____

THE DOORBELL RANG

by Pat Hutchins, Greenwillow, 1989

Nothing tastes as good as home-baked cookies and Ma has made one dozen that she puts on a plate for Sam and Victoria. They look as good as grandma's and they taste as good as grandma's, the children say. Just then the doorbell rings. Two children arrive to share the cookies. Just as they are about to take a bite, the doorbell rings again and again until there many children and not enough cookies to go around. Then the doorbell rings once more. It is grandma to the rescue with a large tray of cookies!

FIND SOMEONE WHO . . .

1. Likes peanut butter cookies better than chocolate chip

   _____

2. Has a grandma who bakes cookies

   _____

3. Has Sam as a first name

   _____

4. Has Victoria as a first name

   _____

5. Has shared cookies with another person

   _____

6. Has answered a doorbell to find a surprise visitor

   _____

7. Can name three different kinds of cookies

   _____

8. Has invited more than three friends to a party

   _____

9. Can name two words that rhyme with RINGS

   _____

10. Knows how many cookies are in a dozen

    _____

DUCK FOR PRESIDENT

by Doreen Cronin; Illus. by Betsy Lewin, Simon & Schuster, 2004

Farmer Brown and all of the animals have a lot of work to do. Duck did not like cutting grass because small blades of grass got caught in his feathers. He decided an election was needed to see who would run the farm. Duck campaigned, registered voters, and won the election. However, Duck found that running a farm was hard work so he decided to run for governor instead. However, Duck found that being governor means lots of hard work. He decided to run for president. He gave speeches, appeared on TV, and won the election. Being president was hard work. Duck hated hard work. He saw a want-ad that said DUCK NEEDED. Back to the farm he went where he wrote his autobiography.

FIND SOMEONE WHO . . .

1. Can name three jobs to do on a farm

   _____

2. Has done a really hard job

   _____

3. Has helped to mow the grass

   _____

4. Knows what an election is

   _____

5. Can name the president of the United States

   _____

6. Can name four animals found on farm

   _____

7. Has had a headache

   _____

8. Has written a story about himself or herself

   _____

9. Can make two new words from the letters in FARMER

   _____

10. Has given a speech

    _____

DUFFY AND THE DEVIL

by Harve Zemach; Illus. by Margot Zemach, Farrar, Straus & Giroux, 1973

Squire Lovel needs a maid to help his old housekeeper and hires lazy, simple-minded Duffy. She claims she can spin and knit but can do neither. Duffy asks the help of the devil to make Squire's clothing. In appreciation for his fine apparel, Squire marries Duffy. But the problems were not over for Duffy and the Squire. The devil must still be paid for the magic clothes. With a little luck and a little magic, the tale ends happily.

FIND SOMEONE WHO . . .

1. Can name two jobs a housekeeper might do

2. Has a first name that begins with the letter D

3. Has a family member who knits

4. Has kept a promise

5. Can name someone who has helped him or her to learn something new

6. Can name someone who did a job he or she was supposed to do

7. Is wearing something that someone made for him or her

8. Can name a job that people pay to have done

9. Can name another story with magic in it

10. Can name another story with a happy ending

ELOISE

by Kay Thompson; Illus. by Hilary Knight,
Simon & Schuster, Reissue 1969

Eloise is a little girl who lives at the Plaza Hotel in New York. She is not yet pretty but she is already a Person. Henry James would want to study her. Queen Victoria would recognize her as an equal. The New York Jets would want to have her on their side. Lewis Carroll would love her. She knows everything about the Plaza. She is interested in people when they are not boring. When there is an open door she walks in and pretends she is an orphan. She helps the busboys set up for luncheons and goes to all the weddings and receptions. She hates school and loves TV and thinks about pouring a pitcher of water down the mail chute. Eloise is six years old and she absolutely loves the Plaza.

FIND SOMEONE WHO . . .

1. Has visited or lived in New York City

   _____

2. Has the first name Eloise, or a first name that begins with the letter E

   _____

3. Can name a hotel in or near your city or town

   _____

4. Has stayed for more than one night in a hotel

   _____

5. Can name a Queen of England

   _____

6. Knows what a busboy is

   _____

7. Can name something written by Lewis Carroll

   _____

8. Has attended a wedding

   _____

9. Likes the TV channel Nickelodeon best

   _____

10. Has a brother or sister who is six years old

    _____

FABLES

by Arnold Lobel, Harper & Row, 1980

Here are 20 fables that teach lessons. A crocodile spends his life in bed because he likes the orderly flowers on his wallpaper rather than the scattered flowers in a garden. Two ducks meet a friendly fox on the road and despite knowing that foxes like to eat ducks, they take the same road again and are nearly caught. In the future they decide to take a different route. A hen sees an apple tree that has grown overnight. It talks and has furry toes. When she tricks the tree into losing its leaves, there stands a wolf. The hen quickly finds safety in her house. A baboon can't close his umbrella. A gibbon tells him to make holes in it. He does and when it rains he gets soaked. Sometimes advice from friends is not always worth heeding.

FIND SOMEONE WHO . . .

1. Has wallpaper with flowers in his or her bedroom

   _____

2. Can name a river where a crocodile swims

   _____

3. Takes the same way home even though a bully is waiting along the way

   _____

4. Can name a story with a fox

   _____

5. Can name a story with an apple tree

   _____

6. Can name three foods made from apples

   _____

7. Has played a trick on someone

   _____

8. Has an umbrella with a hole in it

   _____

9. Has given advice to a friend

   _____

10. Can find a picture of a baboon in the encyclopedia

   _____

THE FAITHFUL FRIEND

by Robert San Souci; Illus. by Brian Pinkney, Simon & Schuster, 1995

Here is a tale from Martinique of two good friends and an evil wizard. Hippolyte lives with his widowed mother and Clement is the son of a wealthy landowner. Clement falls in love with a beautiful maiden's picture and he and his friend set out to meet the lovely Pauline. Clement proposes marriage but the girl's uncle, an evil wizard, places a curse on the couple. Hippolyte discovers what the uncle has done and is determined to protect Clement and Pauline even at the risk of his own life. At last the curses are overcome, the couple is married, and Clement and Hippolyte remain true friends.

FIND SOMEONE WHO . . .

1. Knows where Martinique is located _____

2. Has a friend whose name begins with the letter H _____

3. Has a friend whose name begins with the letter C _____

4. Knows someone with the first name Pauline _____

5. Can name another story with a wizard _____

6. Has attended a wedding _____

7. Can tell about a favor he or she has done for a friend _____

8. Knows what FAITHFUL means _____

9. Has more than one uncle _____

10. Can name one quality of a good friend _____

FERDINAND THE BULL

by Munro Leaf; Illus. by Robert Lawson, Viking, 1936

Ferdinand is a gentle bull who likes to sit and smell the flowers. When men come to pick the fiercest bull for the bullfight, Ferdinand is stung by a bee. He stomps and roars and puffs and snorts. The men think he is the fiercest bull and choose him. What do you think will happen when Ferdinand enters the bull ring?

FIND SOMEONE WHO . . .

1. Likes to be alone part of the time _____

2. Can name three different flowers _____

3. Can find Spain on a map _____

4. Can find an article on Spain in the encyclopedia _____

5. Has been stung by a bee _____

6. Has worn a flower in his lapel or in her hair _____

7. Can say two words that rhyme with SPAIN _____

8. Knows what FIERCE means _____

9. Has run through or played in a meadow _____

10. Has taken part in a parade _____

FIN M'COUL, THE GIANT OF KNOCKMANY HILL

by Tomie dePaola, Holiday House, 1981

No giant was more scared of Cucullin, the strongest giant in Ireland, than Fin M'Coul. Finn escaped Cucullin many times but the threat of being flattened by the giant's thunderbolt remained. One day Fin's wife decided to put an end to Cucullin and prepared a scheme sure to work. When the big giant showed up at Fin's home on Knockmany Hill, he found a baby (who was really Fin) who could eat iron pancakes. He bothered Fin no more.

FIND SOMEONE WHO . . .

1. Can name something found in Ireland _____

2. Can name another story with a giant _____

3. Knows what to avoid in a thunderstorm _____

4. Can name three things bigger than a bus _____

5. Likes pancakes for breakfast _____

6. Has a baby brother or sister _____

7. Knows what kind of word PANCAKES is _____

8. Has climbed a hill _____

9. Can make three other words that rhyme with FIN. _____

10. Has had breakfast in someone else's home _____

FINDERS KEEPERS

by Will & Nicolas, Harcourt, 1951

Suppose you found something you wanted to keep but another person touched it first. Who would it belong to? That is the problem for Nap and Winkle, two dogs who work together to dig up a bone in the yard. Nap sees the bone first but Winkle touches it first. They cannot decide who should get the bone so they find a number of different people to ask. They ask a farmer, a goat, and a barber who should get the bone but get no satisfactory answers. The problem is finally solved when they ask a fellow dog.

FIND SOMEONE WHO . . .

1. Has tried digging for treasure

2. Has found a bone in his or her yard

3. Keeps two dogs as pets

4. Can tell of a time when you and another person both wanted the same thing

5. Has lived on or visited a farm

6. Has had a haircut in a barber shop

7. Can name three animals found on a farm

8. Can say two words that rhyme with NAP

9. Can make two new words from letters found in FARMER

10. Can name someone who has helped solve a problem

FLATFOOT FOX AND THE CASE OF THE MISSING EYE

by Eth Clifford; Illus. by Brian Lies, Houghton Mifflin, 1990

Flatfoot Fox, the smartest detective in the world, was sitting in his office, just waiting for something to happen, when in walked Fat Cat. Fat Cat was mean and Fat Cat was mad and what's more, Fat Cat had a mystery to be solved. Detective Fox and his faithful assistant, Secretary Bird, set out to discover who had been the thief at Fat Cat's birthday party. Flatfoot Fox finds the culprit in true detective style, of course, but before the case is closed the two have met a zany assortment of suspects, starting with a Really Ridiculous Rabbit, and Flatfoot Fox has proved how clever he is.

FIND SOMEONE WHO . . .

1. Has lost something that was never found

   _____

2. Has a big fat cat at home

   _____

3. Knows what a detective does

   _____

4. Has given or attended a birthday party

   _____

5. Has touched a real rabbit

   _____

6. Would like a pig for a pet

   _____

7. Can name one thing a goat would eat

   _____

8. Can say two words that rhyme with FOX

   _____

9. Has blue eyes

   _____

10. Would like to pick up a black snake

   _____

FLOSSIE AND THE FOX

by Patricia McKissack; Illus. by Rachel Isadora, Dial, 1986

Flossie lives with Big Mama in the Piney Woods. One morning Big Mama asks Flossie to take a basket of eggs to Miss Viola at the farm on the other side of the woods. On the way Flossie meets the fox (who loves eggs) who has frightened Miss Viola's chickens so much that they won't lay eggs. In order to get through the woods safely and with all the eggs in her basket, Flossie fools the fox into believing that she doesn't know what kind of creature he is. Fox becomes more and more frustrated trying to convince Flossie that he is, indeed, a fox but to no avail...until the very last moment when she reaches the farm.

FIND SOMEONE WHO . . .

1. Has taken a gift to his or her grandmother _____

2. Has walked alone in the woods _____

3. Likes fried eggs for breakfast _____

4. Has filled a basket with food _____

5. Has lived on or visited a farm _____

6. Has a dog for a pet _____

7. Can name another story with a fox _____

8. Has counted chickens in a barn-yard _____

9. Can name three other animals that live in the woods _____

10. Can name two words that rhyme with FOX _____

FLY AWAY HOME

by Eve Bunting; Illus. by Ronald Himler, Houghton Mifflin, 1991

The only home Andrew and his dad have is the airport. "It's better than the streets," Dad says. "It's warm. It's safe. And the price is right." What Dad says is true. But still, Andrew hopes that one day life will be the way it used to be. Then he and his dad can have a place of their own again. The first rule for living in the airport is not to get noticed. Andrew and his Dad stay with the crowds and change airline waiting areas often. When Andrew sees a small trapped bird fluttering in the high hollow spaces he whispers for it to "Fly away home." When the bird finally does escape, Andrew sees hope for himself and his Dad.

FIND SOMEONE WHO . . .

1. Has spent time in an airport _____

2. Has tried hard not to be noticed _____

3. Has seen a bird trapped in a building _____

4. Has earned money by doing a job _____

5. Knows what a security guard does _____

6. Has pushed a luggage cart in an airport _____

7. Has gone to sleep sitting up _____

8. Knows what a skycap does _____

9. Has flown in an airplane _____

10. Knows someone who works in an airport _____

FOLLOW THE DRINKING GOURD

by *Jeanette Winter*, Knopf, 1988

"Follow the Drinking Gourd" is a song with hidden meaning. In the days of slavery, a handy man named Peg Leg Joe traveled from one plantation to another doing carpenter work with his handy hammer and saw. While he worked he sang a song. The slaves listened carefully to the words for they told of all the landmarks a slave should look for in escaping north to freedom. A slave family learns that they are to be divided and sold but they escape at night following the directions given in the song. They reach the river where a boatman awaits them and they make their way to a safe house where they are given food and shelter. The escape is successful when the family finally arrives in Canada where they can be free.

FIND SOMEONE WHO . . .

1. Knows what a drinking gourd is _____

2. Can explain the purpose of the Underground Railroad _____

3. Has visited or lived in a different country _____

4. Can name another story where someone has escaped _____

5. Can name two famous African Americans _____

6. Can tell which direction Canada is from the United States _____

7. Can draw a picture of the Big Dipper _____

8. Can sing the chorus of "Go Down Moses" _____

9. Knows what a safe house was _____

10. Can make a word from letters in SLAVERY that means 365 days _____

THE FOOL OF THE WORLD AND THE FLYING SHIP

by Arthur Ransome; Illus. by Uri Schulevitz, Farrar,
Straus & Giroux, 1987

There was once a boy who was not considered to be very bright. He had two older brothers. The Czar sends a notice throughout the land that whoever brings him a flying ship shall marry his daughter. The older brothers set off to find the flying ship but are never heard from again. The foolish boy also goes and in his travels he meets a wise old man. After sharing his food, the old man gives the lad some strict instructions on how to find a beautiful flying ship. The fool sets off following the instructions and asks every man he meets on the road to join him. Some of the men are very strange fellows indeed. The fool lands the ship in the Czar's backyard but, not satisfied, the Czar insists that the fool undertake several difficult tasks. With the help of the strange men on the ship the fool accomplishes each task and marries the princess.

FIND SOMEONE WHO . . .

1. Has two older brothers

2. Knows what country a Czar would rule

3. Can give another name for a flying ship

4. Can name another story with a wise older person

5. Has shared his or her lunch with another

6. Can give some good advice to the group

7. Has gone on a long trip

8. Has done a difficult job with the help of others

9. Can give instructions on how to play a game

10. Can give the name of a princess in a story

FREDERICK

by Leo Lionni, Pantheon, 1995

The mouse family was preparing for winter, gathering corn, nuts, wheat, and straw. They worked day and night to store enough food to last through the cold winter months. But Frederick did not gather food or straw. He gathered colors and words that the other mice thought were foolish things to gather. Then winter comes and when the cold seeps through the granary and the food supply is almost gone, Frederick shares his words and colors and the other mice find that these were fine things to store indeed.

FIND SOMEONE WHO . . .

1. Has found a mouse in his or her house

2. Has played when he or she was supposed to be working

3. Can sing a song all the way through

4. Likes winter better than summer

5. Has red as his or her favorite color

6. Has Art as his or her favorite class

7. Likes to listen to stories

8. Has done something to make a person feel better

9. Can recite a poem

10. Knows a word that rhymes with MOUSE

THE FUNNY LITTLE WOMAN

by Arlene Mosel; Illus. by Blair Lent, E.P. Dutton, 1972

A little woman in old Japan liked to make dumplings and liked to laugh, tee-he-he. One day a dumpling rolled through a hole in the floor of her house. When the woman tried to catch it she found herself on a strange road under the Earth. There, the statues of the gods tried to hide the little woman from the wicked Oni. But the little woman laughed and the Oni caught her and took her home. The little woman cooked for the Oni using a paddle that turned one grain of rice into a potful. Then she became lonesome and tried to run away. Will the Oni catch her?

FIND SOMEONE WHO . . .

1. Likes chicken and dumplings for dinner

   _____

2. Can find Japan on a map

   _____

3. Has been in a game of Hide-and-Seek

   _____

4. Has walked or biked down a strange road

   _____

5. Can name a wicked character in another story

   _____

6. Can name a dish made with rice

   _____

7. Can tell a joke that makes people laugh

   _____

8. Has helped cook a meal at home

   _____

9. Can name three things found under the Earth

   _____

10. Can name four words that rhyme with RICE

    _____

THE GARDENER

by Sarah Stewart; Illus. by David Small, Farrar, Straus & Giroux, 1997

Lydia, who lives in the country, must move to the city to live with her Uncle Jim. It is the time of the Great Depression and Lydia's family has fallen on hard times. The city is noisy and dirty. Uncle Jim is kind but he never smiles. Lydia does make friends with the neighbors and with the workers in Uncle Jim's bakery and when spring comes she transforms the rooftop of the apartment building into a garden. Surely when Uncle Jim sees this little bit of the country brought to the city there will be a smile on his face. At least Lydia hopes so.

FIND SOMEONE WHO . . .

1. Has lived in the country

    _____

2. Has lived in a big city

    _____

3. Has been away from home for more than a week

    _____

4. Knows someone with the first name Lydia

    _____

5. Can name three flowers that grow in a garden

    _____

6. Has helped someone plant seeds

    _____

7. Has a bakery near where he or she lives

    _____

8. Has been on the rooftop of an apartment building

    _____

9. Can tell a story to make people smile

    _____

10. Can name three signs of spring

    _____

GEORGE AND MARTHA

by James Marshall, Houghton Mifflin, 1972

When you can't stand split-pea soup and you don't want to hurt your friend Martha's feelings after she's made a pot of it, what else can you do but hide the soup so she thinks you ate it? And if your loafers are the only place available, well, it's all in the name of friendship. Friendship is friendship even if you are a hippopotamus. At least that's the way George looks at things and even though he doesn't fool Martha, all ends happily with chocolate chip cookies instead of split-pea soup. Friendship proves a delicate thing, even when it exists between two not-so-delicate creatures as George and Martha. Loving and lovable a hippopotamus might be, but delicate he is not. Even so, George and Martha seem to know full well the joys and delights of having a friend to cheer you and to care.

FIND SOMEONE WHO . . .

1. Likes pea soup

_____

2. Has seen a real hippopotamus

_____

3. Likes chocolate chip cookies better than cake

_____

4. Has seen a balloon in the sky

_____

5. Has visited the dentist recently

_____

6. Knows what privacy is

_____

7. Has gotten mad at a friend

_____

8. Can name a favorite restaurant

_____

9. Has done a favor for a friend

_____

10. Can name three animals found in a zoo

_____

THE GHOST OF NICHOLAS GREEBE

by Tony Johnston; Illus. by S.D. Schindler, Dial, 1996

"From this night forth I quest, I quest, till all my bones together rest." So chants the ghost of Nicholas Greebe, whose bone has been stolen from its shallow grave on a small New England farm. As the restless ghost haunts the place, lifting pots and pans, spooking animals, and wailing ceaselessly, the lost bone makes a mysterious journey around the world until one night, after 100 years, the bone finds its way back home.

FIND SOMEONE WHO . . .

1. Likes to hear ghost stories   _____

2. Has a small dog for a pet   _____

3. Can find New England on a map   _____

4. Knows what scrimshaw is   _____

5. Can find a picture of a sailing ship   _____

6. Has been on a farm in the past three months   _____

7. Can find Alaska on a map   _____

8. Can name another story about a dog   _____

9. Can name three words that rhyme with STONE   _____

10. Can name four different farm animals   _____

THE GIANT AND THE BEANSTALK

by Diane Stanley, HarperCollins, 2004

For a giant, Otto is embarrassingly polite. While all the other giants are studying cursing, growling, and stomping, Otto just wants to play with his pet hen, Clara. Then one terrible day a wiley human named Jack climbs up the magic beanstalk and steals her away! Knowing only the thief's name, Otto must find Clara and rescue her from the land of fairy tales. The only problem is, there seem to be a lot of Jacks down there. When he finally does find the right Jack he trades a cow for Clara and all ends happily.

FIND SOMEONE WHO . . .

1. Can name a story with a giant _____

2. Can name two words to say when you are being polite _____

3. Has a bird for a pet _____

4. Knows what you would find at the top of a beanstalk _____

5. Knows another word for THIEF _____

6. Has watched someone milk a cow _____

7. Has the first name Jack _____

8. Has a first name that begins with the letter O _____

9. Can name two words that rhyme with HEN _____

10. Can name two other fairy tales _____

THE GIRL WHO LOVED WILD HORSES

by Paul Goble, Atheneum, 1978

The Girl Who Loved Wild Horses is the story of a Native American girl whose people lived on the plains, moved from place to place, and kept horses to carry their belongings and hunt buffalo. The girl loved the horses and understood them in a special way. During a storm, she was carried away by the horses to a strange land where she and the horses were welcomed by a wild stallion. The girl became one with the horses. A year later, when hunters from the girl's tribe found her and took her home, she longed to return to her first love, the horses.

FIND SOMEONE WHO . . .

1. Can name a Native American tribe

   _____

2. Has seen a real buffalo

   _____

3. Has ridden a horse

   _____

4. Has gotten wet in the rain

   _____

5. Is not afraid of storms

   _____

6. Has been away from home for more than a week

   _____

7. Who has lived in more than two places

   _____

8. Knows what a stallion is

   _____

9. Can say two words that rhyme with LAND

   _____

10. Knows what a tipi is

   _____

THE GLORIOUS FLIGHT

by Alice and Martin Provensen, Viking, 1983

The Glorious Flight tells the story of Louis Bleroit (1872–1936), who was one of the truly great pioneers of aviation. He devoted a fortune acquired by his invention of automobile headlamps to the development and construction of a series of airplanes he designed and built himself. On July 25, 1909, this French aviation pioneer made the first flight across the English Channel, flying from France to England in 37 minutes. This was truly a glorious flight.

FIND SOMEONE WHO . . .

1. Knows who pioneered flight in France

   _____

2. Knows who pioneered flight in the United States

   _____

3. Can find France on a map

   _____

4. Can find England on a map

   _____

5. Has built and raced a model car

   _____

6. Has flown a model airplane

   _____

7. Can name three important inventions

   _____

8. Knows how long it takes a passenger plane today to fly from New York to London

   _____

9. Can name the first American to fly solo across the Atlantic Ocean

   _____

10. Can name a famous woman aviator

    _____

GOLDILOCKS AND THE THREE BEARS

by James Marshall, Dial, 1988, Reissue 1996

Here is a fresh retelling of a familiar tale. In this tale Goldilocks is spoiled, stubborn, and often very badly behaved. She takes a shortcut through the woods to go to the village to buy muffins. There are many danger signs that she ignores and she arrives at the house of the three bears. She barges in to find no one there and proceeds to make herself at home, sampling the food, trying the chairs, and taking a nap on one of the beds. When the bears do arrive home they frighten Goldilocks who runs away.

FIND SOMEONE WHO . . .

1. Has walked alone in the woods _____

2. Has seen a real bear at the zoo _____

3. Has a first name that begins with the letter G _____

4. Likes muffins better than doughnuts _____

5. Has had a toy broken by someone else _____

6. Likes hot oatmeal for breakfast _____

7. Can draw a picture of a Danger Sign _____

8. Has spent time in an empty house _____

9. Likes to take a nap in the afternoon _____

10. Can name another fairy tale _____

GOLEM

by David Wisniewski, Clarion, 1996

The Jews of Prague are being falsely accused of terrible deeds and Rabbi Loew knows he must act before people rise up against the Jews. The Rabbi creates a huge clay giant and brings it to life using magical powers. The Golem seeks and finds those who are telling false tales about the Jews and turns the liars in to the authorities. Other enemies of the Jews storm the gates of the ghetto, hoping to destroy all of the Jews and their homes. Once again the Golem comes to the rescue and defeats the enemy using their own battering ram. With the Jews' victory there is no further need for the Golem. The huge clay creature begs the Rabbi to let him live but his pleas are not heeded and the Golem is returned back to its magical land.

FIND SOMEONE WHO . . .

1. Can name a story where someone has been falsely accused

2. Can name a time in history when the Jewish people have been persecuted

3. Knows what a Rabbi is _____

4. Knows what a ghetto is _____

5. Has a last name that begins with the letter L _____

6. Can name a fairy tale where someone has magical powers _____

7. Can name the country where Prague is located _____

8. Has made a creature out of clay _____

9. Can think of something he or she has no further need for _____

10. Can name another story with a magical land _____

GRANDFATHER'S JOURNEY

by Allen Say, Houghton Mifflin, 1993

A young Japanese boy was amazed at the sights he saw when he set forth to see the world. In North America he rode riverboats and trains and often walked to see deserts, open fields, mountains, rivers, and busy cities. When he returned to his homeland, he married and brought his bride to California in the United States. But he never forgot Japan and when his daughter was grown, he took his family to that country. They lived there until the war destroyed his city home, so the family moved to a small village. When his grandson grew up, the boy traveled to the United States and discovered that he had two homes...one in Japan and one in California. He loved both and, just like his grandfather, when he was in one he missed the other.

FIND SOMEONE WHO . . .

1. Has visited another country _____

2. Has counted cars as a train went by _____

3. Has ridden on a riverboat _____

4. Has run across an open field _____

5. Can find California on a map _____

6. Can find Japan on a map _____

7. Has climbed a mountain _____

8. Has lived in or visited a big city _____

9. Has lived in or visited a small town _____

10. Can name four states in the United States _____

THE GREAT KAPOK TREE

by Lynne Cherry, Harcourt, Brace, Jovanovich, 1990

Tired from chopping the huge trunk of the tree, a young man became weary and sat down to rest under the great Kapok tree. The creatures who lived there were concerned because they needed the tree. The bee and the snake used the tree as a home. Others warned that destroying the trees would rob the land. The predators, concerned about their food supply, urged the man to consider carefully before cutting more trees. All who lived there feared for the life of the rain forest. Suddenly, the young man woke from his deep dream. The animals of the rain forest waited and wondered. Would the man leave the rain forest to grow and flourish? Would the animals live there in peace? To find out, read *The Great Kapok Tree.*

FIND SOMEONE WHO . . .

1. Has gone to sleep under a tree   _____

2. Can name two things made from trees   _____

3. Knows what a rain forest is   _____

4. Has seen a real monkey   _____

5. Has walked in a forest   _____

6. Has had a pleasant dream   _____

7. Has a name that begins with the letter K   _____

8. Can say two words that rhyme with RAIN   _____

9. Has done a hard job   _____

10. Has seen a real jaguar   _____

THE GROUCHY LADYBUG

by Eric Carle, Thomas Y. Crowell, 1977

At 5:00 a.m. the grouchy Ladybug meets another ladybug and wants to eat all the aphids on a leaf. After angering the other ladybug, the grouchy Ladybug decides to fight someone bigger. Each hour she meets someone larger than herself: a yellow jacket, a beetle, a praying mantis, and finally a whale. The whale is so huge that she can pick a fight with only one portion of the whale at a time. The whale's tail slaps Ladybug so hard that it sends her flying across the ocean and she lands right back on the leaf with the other ladybug. Still friendly, the other ladybug shares the aphids for dinner.

FIND SOMEONE WHO . . .

1. Can name two colors on a lady-bug

    _____

2. Can name a tree that has leaves

    _____

3. Has felt grouchy more than once

    _____

4. Knows why to avoid a yellow jacket

    _____

5. Has caught a praying mantis

    _____

6. Is the tallest person in the group or class

    _____

7. Knows what a bully is

    _____

8. Can draw a picture of a whale

    _____

9. Can name an ocean he or she has seen

    _____

10. Has shared his or her lunch with someone

    _____

HANSEL AND GRETEL

by Rika Lesser; Illus. by Paul O. Zelinsky, Putnam, 1996

Because a poor family has so little to eat, two of the children are left in the woods to care for themselves. As Hansel and Gretel wander through the woods they come upon a gingerbread house decorated with candy. The house belongs to a witch who puts Hansel in a cage to feed and fatten up and sets Gretel to many household tasks. Gretel fools the witch, whose eyesight is none too good, and manages to push her into an oven. Gretel frees Hansel and the children discover riches in the cottage that they take home with them.

FIND SOMEONE WHO . . .

1. Has a first name that begins with the letter H

   _____

2. Has a first name that begins with the letter G

   _____

3. Has walked in the woods with a brother or sister

   _____

4. Can name a fairy tale with a witch

   _____

5. Can name something you would find in a cage

   _____

6. Has eaten gingerbread cookies

   _____

7. Wears glasses

   _____

8. Can name three things to bake in an oven

   _____

9. Can tell of a time when he or she was lost

   _____

10. Can name a household task he or she does every day

    _____

HAROLD AND THE PURPLE CRAYON

by Crockett Johnson, Harper & Row, 1955, Reprinted in HarperCollins Treasury of Picture Book Classics, 2002

Harold with his purple crayon creates a fantasy walk in the moonlight that takes him through a small forest to an apple tree guarded by a dragon. To escape the dragon Harold heads for the water and climbs in a small boat. Landing on a beach he creates a wonderful picnic lunch along with a moose and a porcupine to eat the leftover pie. He creates a balloon to ease his fall from a mountain and, in searching for his bedroom window, he draws a city full of windows. He meets a helpful policeman and remembers where his bedroom window is. He returns home, climbs into bed, and falls asleep.

FIND SOMEONE WHO . . .

1. Has a purple crayon _____

2. Has taken a walk in the moonlight _____

3. Can name a story with a dragon _____

4. Has gone on a picnic _____

5. Likes pie better than any other dessert _____

6. Can say a word that rhymes with MOOSE _____

7. Has been helped by a policeman _____

8. Can draw a picture of a full moon _____

9. Has been a passenger in a small boat _____

10. Has visited a beach _____

THE HAT

by Jan Brett, G.P. Putnam's Sons, 1997

Suppose you had something on your head that made you look silly and everyone laughed as you walked by. That is exactly what happened to Hedgie the hedgehog when he walked past Lisa's clothesline and a sock got stuck to his prickles. As each of his animal friends remarks on the sock, Hedgie informs them that it is a hat to help him keep warm when the winter snows come. Lisa discovers her sock is missing and finds Hedgie. She retrieves the sock, telling him that animals do not wear clothing. When she returns to the clothesline where she has hung her winter woolens out, she finds most of them gone. Each farm animal has decided that a hat would be a nice thing to have.

FIND SOMEONE WHO . . .

1. Can give three reasons for wearing a hat

    _____

2. Can name four things that make people laugh

    _____

3. Has lived on or visited a farm

    _____

4. Likes winter better than spring, summer, or fall

    _____

5. Has seen a real hedgehog

    _____

6. Has a clothesline in his or her back yard

    _____

7. Can name two things to do to get ready for winter

    _____

8. Has lost his or her hat

    _____

9. Can name three words that rhyme with SOCK

    _____

10. Has worn two socks that don't match

    _____

HECKEDY PEG

by Audrey Wood; Illus. by Don Wood, Harcourt, 1987

A mother has seven children named Monday, Tuesday, Wednesday, Thursday, Friday, Saturday, and Sunday. She goes into town promising to bring each child a gift if they will not let strangers into the house or play with fire. The children forget her warnings when Heckedy Peg offers them gold to let her in and light her pipe. She turns each child into a food, puts the food in her sack, and takes them with her. When the mother arrives home, she is told by a little bird what happened, and she sets off to rescue her children. The only way she can do this is to guess which food each child has become. Do you think she can do it? Can you?

FIND SOMEONE WHO . . .

1. Has a first name with eight letters

2. Can name two fairy tales with witches

3. Can name two chores he or she does at home

4. Has lived on or visited a farm

5. Can name a story in which a spell was put on someone

6. Can name a crop that might be growing in a field

7. Has been lost at least once

8. Has gotten in trouble because of not minding parents

9. Has crawled through a door on hands and knees

10. Can name the days of the week backwards beginning with Monday

THE HELLO, GOODBYE WINDOW

by Norton Juster; Illus. by Chris Raschka, Hyperion, 2005

A little girl visits her grandparents (Nanna and Poppy) in a big house in the middle of town. All the comings and goings can be seen from the kitchen window called the Hello, Goodbye Window. The little girl loves the kitchen with a table to color on, drawers to take stuff out of, and pictures of the olden days. Poppy plays the harmonica and Nanna turns off the lights and says goodnight to the stars. The girl helps Nanna in the garden, rides her bike, collects sticks and acorns, and kicks a ball around. It is fun imagining what could be coming up to the window...Tyrannosaurus Rex, the pizza delivery guy, or the Queen of England. When her parents come and it is time to leave the little girl feels happy to see her parents but sad to leave Poppy and Nanna.

FIND SOMEONE WHO . . .

1. Has stayed overnight with a grandparent _____

2. Has a grandfather who plays an instrument _____

3. Likes to color at the kitchen table _____

4. Has drawn pictures while sitting at a window _____

5. Has wished on a star _____

6. Has helped someone in a garden _____

7. Can name three things that grow in a garden _____

8. Likes oatmeal best for breakfast _____

9. Has collected sticks and acorns _____

10. Likes to take a nap _____

HERSHEL AND THE HANUKKAH GOBLINS

by Eric Kimmel; Illus. by Trina Schart Hyman, Holiday House, 1989

What are the poor villagers to do? The holiday-hating, hill-dwelling hobgoblins are bound and determined to ruin yet another Hanukkah for them. Every year the beasties snuff out the menorah candles, destroy the dreidels, and pitch the potato latkes on the floor. But these wicked wet blankets never counted on someone as clever as Hershel of Ostropol showing up. Using his wits and a few props—pickles, eggs, and a dreidel (a square-shaped top with Hebrew letters on each side)—Hershel manages to outwit all the creepy critters and break the spell.

FIND SOMEONE WHO . . .

1. Lives or has lived in a small village

2. Knows someone who does not like holidays

3. Knows how many candles are in a menorah

4. Can draw a picture of a goblin

5. Knows what a wet blanket is

6. Has helped make potato latkes

7. Can name another story with a hero

8. Has a first name that begins with the letter H

9. Can name three ways to cook eggs

10. Knows where pickles come from

HEY, AL

by Arthur Yorinks; Illus. by Richard Egielski,
Farrar, Straus & Giroux, 1986

Al, a poor janitor, lives in one room with his dog, Eddie. Eddie is tired of being poor and longs for a better life. He gets his wish when Al is visited by a large bird who promises to take Al and Eddie to a place where they can have everything they desire and where there is no work. At first Al and Eddie enjoy the beautiful place where they can eat and drink and swim whenever they wish. Then one day Al discovers that their noses are beginning to look like beaks. They are slowly turning into birds. As the two escape Al believes that Eddie has drowned in the ocean and is very sad. But the two are eventually reunited and discover that friendship is the best gift of all.

FIND SOMEONE WHO . . .

1. Knows what a janitor does

   _____

2. Has a dog for a pet

   _____

3. Can name a bird larger than a robin

   _____

4. Can swim without stopping for five minutes

   _____

5. Can name three important things to take on a trip

   _____

6. Has traveled to another country

   _____

7. Can make four words using the letters in JANITOR

   _____

8. Has jobs he or she must do at home

   _____

9. Has visited or lived in a big city

   _____

10. Has a basement in his or her house

    _____

HONDO AND FABIAN

by Peter McCarty, Holt, 2002

Here is the simple, daily life a dog and cat who live with a family. The parents are never seen but Fabian, the cat, who plays with the baby, often finds it necessary to dive for cover. When not dodging the baby, Fabian unwinds the toilet paper. Hondo, the dog, takes a trip to the beach in the family car where he romps with a canine pal, diving in and out of the waves. At the end of the day Hondo and Fabian eat dinner (each having his own bowl) and, "full and fat," they settle down for the night.

FIND SOMEONE WHO . . .

1. Has a dog and a cat at home
   _____

2. Has a baby brother or sister
   _____

3. Has made sand castles at the beach
   _____

4. Has a pet whose name begins with the letter H
   _____

5. Has a pet whose name begins with the letter F
   _____

6. Has a family car more than ten years old
   _____

7. Knows what a canine is
   _____

8. Has had waves tickle his or her toes at the beach
   _____

9. Can name three words that rhyme with CAT
   _____

10. Can name two words that rhyme with DOG
    _____

HOOWAY FOR WODNEY WAT

by Helen Lester; Illus. by Lynn Munsinger, Houghton Mifflin, 1999

Wodney Wat had a problem. He could not pronounce words that began with or contained the letter R. Wodney's friends don't seem to mind. The rodents in Miss Fuzzleworth's class got along fine until the day Camilla Capybara showed up. She bragged that she was bigger, meaner, and smarter than anyone in the class. The small rodents trembled in fright. For afternoon recess Wodney is chosen to be the leader of Simon Says. His directions to weed the sign, wake the leaves, and go west are easily understood by his classmates. Camilla, however, tries to pull up weeds, wake up the leaves, and finally head west never to be seen again. Wodney Wat saves the day and becomes a hero. A delightful David and Goliath story.

FIND SOMEONE WHO . . .

1. Can name something that is hard to do

   _____

2. Knows what to say if he or she bumps into someone

   _____

3. Can name five good words to describe a rat

   _____

4. Has seen a real rat

   _____

5. Has been teased by a bully

   _____

6. Can explain what a hero is

   _____

7. Can name one way to show you are brave

   _____

8. Likes baseball better than any other game

   _____

9. Has played the game Simon Says

   _____

10. Can name another story with a bully

   _____

HORTON HATCHES THE EGG

by Dr. Seuss, Random House, 1940

In this tale of faithfulness and responsibility, Mayzie, the lazy bird, takes off for a vacation leaving Horton, the elephant, to sit on her nest. Horton sits through the fall and through the ice and snow of winter for an elephant's faithful 100 percent. When spring comes, hunters capture Horton and sell him to a circus, tree, nest, and all. While he is on display Mayzie happens to fly by. She stops to chat just as the egg begins to break apart. Now Mayzie wants to claim the offspring even though she did none of the work in hatching it. How Dr. Seuss solves the problem of custody makes for a satisfying ending.

FIND SOMEONE WHO . . .

1. Likes scrambled eggs for breakfast

   _____

2. Has gone to a circus

   _____

3. Has seen a real elephant

   _____

4. Has gone on vacation to another state

   _____

5. Has found a bird's nest on the ground

   _____

6. Can name a lazy character in a story

   _____

7. Likes winter better than any other season

   _____

8. Can make three new words from the letters in HORTON

   _____

9. Can explain what FAITHFUL means

   _____

10. Can name three other circus animals

    _____

HOT AIR: THE (MOSTLY) TRUE STORY OF
THE FIRST HOT AIR BALLOON RIDE

by Marjorie Priceman, Atheneum, 2005

On September 19, 1783 thousands of people have gathered on the lawns of the palace in Versailles in France. They have come to watch an amazing event: a hot air balloon will rise into the air. Joseph and Etienne Montgolfier have worked for months to get ready for the flight. The passengers on this first ride into the sky are a sheep, a hen, and a rooster. The balloon takes off, crosses a clothesline, and soars above church steeples. A flock of birds circles the basket and the duck falls and lands in a fountain below. She takes wing and soon is back in the air. Another bird pops the balloon with her beak and the basket descends into the woods with all passengers safe.

FIND SOMEONE WHO . . .

1. Can find France on a map _____

2. Has seen a hot air balloon in the sky _____

3. Can draw a picture of a hot air balloon _____

4. Can name four people who might live in a palace _____

5. Can name something thousands of people like to watch _____

6. Knows what kind of cloth we get from sheep _____

7. Has gathered eggs from a hen's nest _____

8. Has fallen into water _____

9. Has ridden in an airplane _____

10. Can name a church that has a steeple _____

HOT-AIR HENRY

by Mary Calhoun; Illus. by Erich Ingraham, William Morrow, 1981

A Siamese cat named Henry accidentally takes off in a hot air balloon, leaving the Man and the Kid far below. As he sails out over the countryside Henry enjoys the dizzying heights but learns there is more to ballooning than watching the clouds go by. Before the fur-raising flight is over, he and his balloon are put at the mercy of a sharp-beaked eagle, flown into a flock of honking hissing geese, and led dangerously close to high power lines. It is a breathtaking journey.

FIND SOMEONE WHO . . .

1. Has a cat for a pet

   _____

2. Has a first or middle name of Henry

   _____

3. Has seen a hot air balloon in the sky

   _____

4. Has flown in an airplane

   _____

5. Has seen a real eagle

   _____

6. Has watched a flock of geese in the sky

   _____

7. Can tell why to stay away from a high power line

   _____

8. Can name three things that are very hot

   _____

9. Can say five words that rhyme with CAT

   _____

10. Can name another story with a cat

    _____

A HOUSE IS A HOUSE FOR ME

by Mary Ann Hoberman; Illus. by Betty Fraser, Viking, 1978

Here is a book written in lilting, rhythmic verse that describes all kinds of houses...houses for people, houses for animals, and very unusual houses. A glove is a house for a hand. A mirror is a house for reflections... And after naming as many kinds of houses as she can, the author lets us know that the Earth is a house for us all. The illustrations show the many objects and creatures that share the Earth as home and provide a springboard for the reader to think about his or her responsibility for keeping the Earth as clean as a home should be.

FIND SOMEONE WHO . . .

1. Can name a house for a bird

   _____

2. Can name a house for crackers

   _____

3. Can name a house for the head

   _____

4. Can say a word that rhymes with HOUSE

   _____

5. Can tell two ways to help keep the Earth clean

   _____

6. Helps at home cleaning the house

   _____

7. Knows who built a house of sticks

   _____

8. Can name a story about a house

   _____

9. Can name a house for animals

   _____

10. Has a dog house in his or her yard

    _____

THE HUNDRED DRESSES

by Eleanor Estes; Illus. by Louis Slobodkin, Harcourt, 1944

Wanda wore the same faded blue dress to school every day. It was always clean but sometimes it looked as though it had been washed and never ironed. Peggy started the game of the dresses when suddenly one day Wanda said, "I have a hundred dresses at home—all lined up in my closet." After that it was fun to stop Wanda on the way to school and ask, "How many dresses did you say you have?" "A hundred," she would answer. Then everyone laughed and Wanda's lips would tighten as she walked off with one shoulder hunched up in a way none of the girls understood. Wanda did have the hundred dresses, and this is the story of how Peggy and Maddie came to understand about them and about what their game had meant to Wanda.

FIND SOMEONE WHO . . .

1. Walks to school

    _____

2. Does not like to read in front of the class

    _____

3. Knows what DILAPIDATED means

    _____

4. Has gotten in trouble for daydreaming

    _____

5. Has teased someone else

    _____

6. Has been teased by someone

    _____

7. Likes to draw

    _____

8. Has won a contest

    _____

9. Likes the color blue best

    _____

10. Has moved from one town to another

    _____

IF YOU GIVE A MOOSE A MUFFIN

by Laura Joffe Numeroff; Illus. by Felicia Bond, HarperCollins, 1991

Get ready for all kinds of fun if you give a muffin to a moose. He may want to go to the store for some jam, ask to borrow a sweater, sew on a button, make sock puppets, put on a puppet show, pretend to be a Halloween ghost, spill paints that have to be cleaned up, and generally make a mess of things. But all ends well when muffins and mother's homemade blackberry jam come together. Here is a funny introduction to the way an author uses cause and effect in a story. One event leads to the next and to the next in the adventures of moose and his friend. Finally the circular story ends at the place where it began.

FIND SOMEONE WHO . . .

1. Has seen a real moose _____

2. Likes muffins for breakfast _____

3. Has lost a button _____

4. Has seen a puppet show _____

5. Has picked berries _____

6. Has a clothesline in his or her yard _____

7. Can name a word creature that rhymes with MOOSE _____

8. Has been a ghost on Halloween _____

9. Can name a story with a ghost _____

10. Has made a mess using paints _____

IF YOU GIVE A MOUSE A COOKIE

by Laura Joffe Numeroff; Illus. by Felicia Bond, HarperCollins, 1985

Giving a mouse a cookie should be a simple matter but it does lead to complications in this story. Cookies and milk go together so of course the mouse has to have some milk. In wiping the milk off his whiskers he realizes that the whiskers need a trim and after trimming he sweeps up with a broom. Before he can have a nap he must have a story and the story is so exciting that he must draw a picture of it. When the picture is displayed on the refrigerator the mouse realizes that he is hungry again and must have a cookie with, of course, a glass of milk to go with it.

FIND SOMEONE WHO . . .

1. Likes peanut butter cookies better than chocolate chip cookies

   _____

2. Has swept up crumbs with a broom

   _____

3. Can name a story that has been read to your class or group

   _____

4. Likes to draw pictures

   _____

5. Does not like mice

   _____

6. Can say a Mother Goose rhyme about a mouse

   _____

7. Can name another story about a mouse

   _____

8. Can say a word that rhymes with BROOM

   _____

9. Can change one letter in MOUSE to tell where the mouse lives

   _____

10. Does not like to take a nap

   _____

I'M IN CHARGE OF CELEBRATIONS

by Byrd Baylor; Illus. by Peter Parnall, Simon & Schuster, 1986

Can one be lonely in the desert? Not if you see all of the things to celebrate! Celebrate Dust Devil Day when the desert sands swirl in the wind and create a triple rainbow; Coyote Day celebrates the answering calls of the desert coyote; there is a time of Falling Stars and New Year Day and many other days to celebrate if one has eyes and ears open to delight in the wonders of the desert. The author says you will know it is time to celebrate when your heart will pound and you'll feel like you are standing on top of a mountain and you'll catch your breath like you were breathing some new kind of air.

FIND SOMEONE WHO . . .

1. Has visited or lived in the desert _____

2. Has been caught in a dust storm _____

3. Can name three beautiful things in nature _____

4. Can name four colors of a rainbow _____

5. Has heard coyotes howl _____

6. Has seen a falling star _____

7. Can name one desert in the United States _____

8. Has climbed a mountain _____

9. Can name three desert animals _____

10. Can name three days to celebrate in a forest _____

IMOGENE'S ANTLERS

by David Small, Crown Publishers, 1985

Suppose you woke up one morning to discover you had acquired part of an animal! This is what happens to Imogene when she awakens to find she has sprouted antlers. They do cause SOME difficulty for her in getting dressed and going through doors. Her mother's reaction at the sight of her daughter with antlers is to faint. None of the experts consulted could help Imogene but she did discover that antlers have some useful purposes. Imogene's problem is finally solved, or is it?

FIND SOMEONE WHO . . .

1. Can name an animal with antlers _____

2. Has awakened to a surprise _____

3. Can name a time when his or her mother has been excited _____

4. Knows what looking on the bright side means _____

5. Has received something he or she didn't need _____

6. Can name an unusual Christmas decoration _____

7. Can name one good thing about having peacock feathers _____

8. Knows what an encyclopedia is _____

9. Has a bird feeder in his or her yard _____

10. Can name the principal of a school _____

IN THE SMALL, SMALL POND

by Denise Fleming, Holt, 1993

Life in a small pond is fascinating as the creatures who live in and around the pond wiggle, waddle, hover, swoop, and swirl through the seasons of the year. Fish, frogs, and fowl move about in the tall green grass and yellow flowers of spring and summer, then on through falling leaves of fall and, finally, in a barren, frozen landscape as "Chill breeze, winter freeze" sets in. Told in rhyming couplets, here is a young child's introduction to wildlife that is never still.

FIND SOMEONE WHO . . .

1. Has a pond in or near his or her yard

   _____

2. Has caught a frog near a pond

   _____

3. Has watched geese fly down to a pond

   _____

4. Can tell what a tadpole will become

   _____

5. Can tell three signs of autumn

   _____

6. Knows where frogs go in the winter

   _____

7. Can name two creatures who come to a pond to drink

   _____

8. Can name a pond creature that rhymes with DISH

   _____

9. Likes winter better than any other season

   _____

10. Has hidden in tall grass

   _____

JOHN HENRY

by Julius Lester; Illus. by Jerry Pinkney, Dial, 1994

When John Henry is born animals come from near and far to see him. It is evident that this is a most unusual baby who is destined for great things. While still a child he works with his father adding a wing on a house as well as a swimming pool in one morning. Born with a hammer in his hand, John Henry as a young man is set in a race to tunnel through a mountain faster than a modern steam drill. He hammered so hard and so fast and so long that his big heart burst, and the astounded onlookers learned that the way you live your life is mor e important than the ending of it.

FIND SOMEONE WHO . . .

1. Can name two tall tale heroes

    _____

2. Has the first name of JOHN

    _____

3. Has ridden through a tunnel

    _____

4. Has won a race

    _____

5. Who has the initials J.H.

    _____

6. Has taken a trip to the mountains

    _____

7. Has fixed something with a hammer

    _____

8. Has watched a craftsman at work

    _____

9. Has watched men at work building a house

    _____

10. Has a swimming pool at or near his or her home

    _____

JOSEPH HAD A LITTLE OVERCOAT

by *Simms Taback,* Viking, 1999

When Joseph's favorite overcoat gets old and worn, he makes a jacket out of it. When the jacket is more patches than jacket, Joseph turns it into a vest. When the vest is tattered and torn Joseph makes a scarf. The scarf becomes a handkerchief and the handkerchief is used to cover a button. When the button is lost it seems that Joseph can make nothing else...or can he? Yes! Joseph does manage to make something out of nothing.

FIND SOMEONE WHO . . .

1. Is wearing something made by a family member

   _____

2. Is wearing something an older brother once wore

   _____

3. Has a patch on his or her jeans

   _____

4. Can name a new use for a plastic egg carton

   _____

5. Has the first name JOE or JOSEPH

   _____

6. Has a younger brother who wears something he or she once wore

   _____

7. Knows what it means to recycle

   _____

8. Has lost a button from a coat

   _____

9. Knows someone who is a tailor

   _____

10. Has more than one grandfather

   _____

JULIUS, THE BABY OF THE WORLD

by Kevin Henkes, Greenwillow, 1990

Julius is the baby of the world, his parents believe. But Lilly, his older sister, disagrees. She thought he was disgusting. She hoped he would go away but he didn't. He stayed and stayed and stayed. Nothing her parents said or did could change Lilly's mind about Julius. Then Cousin Garland shows up. "Julius is disgusting with a wet pink nose and beady black eyes," Garland said. Then Lilly has second thoughts. After all, who will defend a little brother if not his older sister!

FIND SOMEONE WHO . . .

1. Has a boy's first name that begins with the letter J

   _____

2. Has a baby brother

   _____

3. Has an older sister

   _____

4. Has had to take care of a younger brother or sister

   _____

5. Has a girl's first name that begins with the letter L

   _____

6. Has a cousin whose name begins with the letter G

   _____

7. Has been kept awake by a baby crying

   _____

8. Has helped a younger brother who was being picked on

   _____

9. Has beautiful brown eyes

   _____

10. Is the oldest child in the family

   _____

JUMANJI

by Chris Van Allsburg, Houghton Mifflin, 1981

Peter and Judy were bored and looking for something interesting to do. The game they found under the tree looked like others they had at home, but they decided to give it a try. Little did they know that their quiet house would be taken over by an exotic jungle. The directions stated that once the game is started it wouldn't be over until one player reaches the Golden City. Peter and Judy were in for more excitement than they bargained for.

FIND SOMEONE WHO . . .

1. Can name a board game that uses dice

2. Has a piano at home

3. Has seen a real lion

4. Can name a book that contains nothing but maps

5. Knows another story about a mischievous monkey

6. Has a home near a park

7. Knows what a volcano is

8. Has seen a rhinoceros at the zoo

9. Has seen a python at the zoo

10. Has made a mess in the kitchen

KATY NO-POCKET

by Emmy Payne; Illus. by H. A. Rey, Houghton Mifflin, 1944

Imagine a mother kangaroo without a pocket. Where will she carry her baby? This is Katy No-Pocket's problem. Her baby, Freddy, needs a warm pocket to ride in when Katy goes from one place to another. All the other mother kangaroos have pockets for their babies so Katy has to find one. First she asks other animals how they carry their babies but none of their suggestions seems right for Katy. Finally the owl suggests that she might be able to buy a pocket in the city so off Katy goes. Sure enough, she meets a man wearing all kinds of pockets in a big apron. One of them is just right for Freddy and Katy is delighted when the man gives her his apron. When Katy gets home she decides to make use of all her extra pockets by carrying as many of the little animals as she can.

FIND SOMEONE WHO . . .

1. Can tell why a mother kangaroo needs a pocket

   _____

2. Has a younger brother or sister

   _____

3. Has pants with no pockets

   _____

4. Knows why an apron is handy for cooking

   _____

5. Has helped someone solve a problem

   _____

6. Has spent a day in the city

   _____

7. Has spent a day at the zoo

   _____

8. Has seen a train go by

   _____

9. Can name three animals that live in the woods

   _____

10. Can make three new words using the letters in POCKET

    _____

THE KEEPING QUILT

by Patricia Polacco, Simon & Schuster, 1988

Leaving the land where you have grown up and coming to a new country and learning a new language and new ways of doing things can be difficult. Great Grandma Anna came to America from Russia. She was very poor and had only the dress she wore and her babushka or head covering. Because she was a growing girl the time came when her beloved dress was too small for her to wear any longer. But the dress was not given away. Anna's mother took not only Anna's dress, but cut into pieces Uncle Vladimir's shirt, Aunt Havalah's nightdress, and Aunt Natasha's apron and with the help of her lady friends she made a beautiful quilt. Anna would still have bits of the dress she loved but as part of a lovely quilt that would be used in many ways in the years to come.

FIND SOMEONE WHO . . .

1. Has Ann or Anna as a first name   _____

2. Has traveled to or lived in another country   _____

3. Can say a few words in another language   _____

4. Has a favorite piece of clothing that is too small to wear   _____

5. Has an aunt and an uncle   _____

6. Has a quilt on his or her bed   _____

7. Has been a new pupil in a school   _____

8. Knows what a babushka is   _____

9. Has more than one grandma   _____

10. Can make a picture out of scraps of paper   _____

KING BIDGOOD'S IN THE BATHTUB

by Audrey Wood; Illus. by Don Wood, Harcourt, 1985

King Bidgood liked his bathtub. In fact, he liked it so much that he refused to get out of it. All day long a young page cries for help from the court to get the king out of the tub. The queen suggests lunch. "We will lunch in the tub," roars the king. A knight calls the king to battle. A duke suggests fishing. The entire court invites the king to a party but none of these ideas work. Night comes and the king is still in the tub. At last the page has an idea: he pulls the plug and solves the problem.

FIND SOMEONE WHO . . .

1. Can name a king in a Mother Goose rhyme

   _____

2. Can name a story with a Queen

   _____

3. Has made a castle out of blocks

   _____

4. Likes peanut butter sandwiches for lunch

   _____

5. Can name two words that rhyme with KING

   _____

6. Can make three new words from the letters in BATTLE

   _____

7. Has caught a fish

   _____

8. Has invited friends to a party

   _____

9. Has ridden a horse

   _____

10. Can name a real queen who lives today

    _____

KITTEN'S FIRST FULL MOON

by Kevin Henkes, Greenwillow, 2004

Kitten is quite new to the world and has yet to enjoy all of the outdoor sights and sounds. It is evening and kitten has taken a stroll from the porch of the home where she lives. Suddenly she sees the moon. Kitten is sure that it must be a bowl of milk in the sky. Kitten is thirsty. Perhaps if she opens her mouth wide, the milk would fall from the sky. Unfortunately the only thing that falls from the sky is a bug. Kitten tries reaching the milk from the top of the tallest tree. Still that bowl of milk remained in the sky. When kitten looked down from the tree to the pond she saw another bowl of milk. She jumped down from the tree and leaped into the pond. The bowl of milk disappeared and kitten crawled out wet and still hungry. As the unhappy kitten once again reaches the porch of her home what does she find there but a bowl of milk!

FIND SOMEONE WHO . . .

1. Likes milk better than any other drink

   _____

2. Has a cat for a pet

   _____

3. Can draw a picture of a full moon

   _____

4. Has fished in a pond

   _____

5. Likes to take a walk in the evening

   _____

6. Can name three things that fall from the sky

   _____

7. Has had a bug in his or her mouth

   _____

8. Has tried to catch something that got away

   _____

9. Can say a word that rhymes with KITTEN

   _____

10. Has climbed a tree

   _____

KOALA LOU

by Mem Fox; Illus. by Pamela Lofts, Harcourt, 1989

Koala Lou was the pride and joy of her parents. One hundred times a day her mother would tell her how much she loved her. Then Koala Lou's brothers and sisters were born and mother was so busy looking after the little ones that she did not have time for Koala Lou. To get her mother's attention, Koala Lou decides to enter the Bush Olympics. She practices and practices to be ready for the big event. However, it is Koala Klaws who wins the tree climbing contest and Koala Lou is heartbroken. She returns to her spot in the blue gum tree late at night, to find her mother waiting for her with a hug and the longed-for words, "Oh, Koala Lou, I do love you."

FIND SOMEONE WHO . . .

1. Has seen a real koala bear   _____

2. Has a brother and a sister   _____

3. Can find Australia on a map   _____

4. Has come in first in a race   _____

5. Has watched the Olympic Games on television   _____

6. Has come in second in a race   _____

7. Knows what practice makes perfect means   _____

8. Has climbed a tree   _____

9. Knows what time of year it is right now in Australia   _____

10. Has to practice something for 30 minutes each day   _____

LEGEND OF THE BLUEBONNET

by Tomie dePaola, G.P. Putnam's Sons, 1983

The rain had not come in a long time. The land was dry and the Commanche people danced for the Great Spirits. A small girl, who had no family, was cared for by the people. Clinging to her doll, she watched as the people danced and prayed for rain to come so that there would be grass. Without green grass, the buffalo would die and the people would have no food. One wise man of the people went to the mountains in hope of hearing the message of the Great Spirits. The Spirits told of how the Earth had been abused by the people. The young girl listened as he described how a sacrifice must be made so that the rains would come. It must be something of more value to the people than anything they own. What would satisfy the Great Spirits? What could the people give so that the rains would fall to the Earth? To find out, read *Legend of the Bluebonnet.*

FIND SOMEONE WHO . . .

1. Can name a Native American tribe

   _____

2. Knows what a drought is

   _____

3. Can name two ways to keep the Earth clean

   _____

4. Has seen a real buffalo

   _____

5. Can tell why rain is important

   _____

6. Can perform a dance for the group

   _____

7. Can name something of real value

   _____

8. Has climbed a mountain

   _____

9. Knows what a sacrifice is

   _____

10. Has watered a garden

   _____

LEGEND OF THE INDIAN PAINTBRUSH

by Tomie dePaola, G.P. Putnam's Sons, 1988

A very small Plains Indian boy longed to grow tall and strong and to join the brave warriors and hunters. But he was too small to keep up with the other boys and was not strong at all. He was not consoled by the wise shaman of the tribe who told him that he would be remembered by the People for another reason. After a time, as the boy grew, he had a vision in which an old man and a young girl spoke to him, telling him that it was his task to paint the deeds of the warriors and the visions of the shamans. The boy then became the recorder of the tribe's history but was not satisfied with the dull colors with which he had to work. The vision came again and he was told where to find his colors. He followed the directions and found brushes filled with paint that allowed him to create the sunset in vivid color. When his painting was finished, he left the brushes behind and the next morning the hill was filled with color as the brushes had taken root in the earth.

FIND SOMEONE WHO . . .

1. Is the smallest person in his or her family

   _____

2. Does not like to play any sport

   _____

3. Has done something to worry a parent

   _____

4. Knows what a shaman is

   _____

5. Can name another Native American story

   _____

6. Has painted a picture

   _____

7. Can describe a pleasant dream

   _____

8. Can name three colors in a sunset

   _____

9. Can tell of a job he or she helped someone do

   _____

10. Likes to write stories

   _____

LEO THE LATE BLOOMER

by Robert Kraus; Illus. by Jose Aruego, Windmill Books, 1971, Re-printed in HarperCollins Treasury of Picture Book Classics, 2002

Poor Leo couldn't do any of the things expected of him. He could not read or write or draw or talk and he was a very messy eater. Leo's father worried about his lack of progress but his mother kept insisting that Leo was just a late bloomer. Even so, time passed and fall became winter and Leo showed no signs of blooming. Finally when spring arrived Leo began to bloom. He could read read, write, and draw and even ate neatly. When he finally spoke it was to say, "I made it."

FIND SOMEONE WHO . . .

1. Could read in kindergarten

   _____

2. Likes to write stories

   _____

3. Never has spilled a glass of milk

   _____

4. Can draw a picture of a flower

   _____

5. Can name something fun to do in the fall

   _____

6. Can name something fun to do in the winter

   _____

7. Can give three ways we know spring is coming

   _____

8. Knows what a late bloomer is

   _____

9. Knows where one can see a real tiger

   _____

10. Has read a whole book alone

   _____

THE LEPRECHAUN'S GOLD

by Pamela Duncan Edwards; Illus. by Henry Cole,
HarperCollins, 2004

Old Pat was the best harpist in the small Irish village. People came from verywhere to hear him. Young Tom wanted to learn to play the harp and Old Pat kindly consented to teach the boy. It happened that a contest was announced to determine the best harpist in all of Ireland. Old Pat decided to enter the contest just for the joy of making music. Young Tom wanted to win the contest for the prize money. They traveled together and one night while Old Pat was asleep, Young Tom broke a string on Old Pat's harp. Pat is awakened by a cry for help and goes to help a leprechaun while Tom runs away. Guess who wins the contest when the grateful leprechaun and his friends arrive to help!

FIND SOMEONE WHO . . .

1. Has Pat or Patrick as a first name

2. Has won something in a contest

3. Is learning to play an instrument

4. Knows what color goes with Ireland

5. Can draw a picture of a harp

6. Knows what leprechauns like to hide

7. Has had to ask someone for help

8. Likes music class better than any other class

9. Has the first name of Tom or Thomas

10. Has spent at least one night outdoors

LILLY'S PURPLE PLASTIC PURSE

by *Kevin Henkes,* Greenwillow, 1996

Lilly loved everything about school, the pencils and chalk, her desk, the shiny hallways, school lunches, and her teacher. At home she played school with her brother, Julius. Yes, school was a wonderful place to be until the day she took her new glittery glasses and purple plastic purse to school. She was so anxious to share her new things that she ignored her teacher's warning to wait and interrupted the class to show off her new things. When her teacher, Mr. Slinger, took the things to keep for her until the end of the day, Lilly was furious. She drew a terrible picture of Mr. Slinger and added terrible words to it and put it into his book bag. At the end of the day Mr. Slinger gave Lilly her purse and glasses to take home. When she looked in her purse she found a note from her teacher and what it said made Lilly ashamed of what she had done. But it was too late to get the picture back. What could she do?

FIND SOMEONE WHO . . .

1. Was given a shiny new quarter _____

2. Has had a man as a first grade teacher _____

3. Has played school with a younger brother or sister _____

4. Wears glasses _____

5. Has gone shopping with a grandparent _____

6. Likes math better than any other subject _____

7. Likes to draw pictures of people _____

8. Takes a book bag to school _____

9. Likes Cheez-Its as a tasty snack _____

10. Has had something taken away by a teacher _____

THE LITTLE HOUSE

by Virginia Lee Burton, Houghton Mifflin, 1942

The little house sat on a hill in the countryside and was happy watching the changing seasons and the activities she saw with each. The farmer planted and harvested his crops. In the summer the children swam in the pond and in the fall they went to school. She liked watching the children on their sleds in the winter and seeing the apple trees bloom in the spring. But roads were built, surveyors came and soon houses, then tall buildings and a whole city grew up around her. She missed the daisies and the apple trees and seeing the children at play. She was forgotten until one day a lady saw her. The lady had played in the house as a child. She bought the house and had it moved to the country where once again the little house could watch the seasons come and go.

FIND SOMEONE WHO . . .

1. Lives or has lived in the country   _____

2. Can name the season crops are
   harvested in   _____

3. Has gone swimming in a pond   _____

4. Has gone sledding in the snow   _____

5. Has picked apples from a tree   _____

6. Has lived in a big city   _____

7. Can name two wildflowers   _____

8. Can name the four seasons   _____

9. Can name two crops farmers
   grow   _____

10. Can say two words that mean
    LITTLE   _____

THE LITTLE OLD LADY WHO WAS NOT AFRAID OF ANYTHING

by Linda Williams; Illus. by Megan Lloyd, HarperCollins, 1986

Once upon a time there was a little old lady who was not afraid of anything. Until one windy autumn night, while walking in the woods, she hears CLOMP CLOMP. "I'm not afraid of you," says the little old lady. But the noises keep growing. CLOMP CLOMP, WIGGLE WIGGLE, SHAKE SHAKE, CLAP CLAP ... and the little old lady who was not afraid of anything has the scare of her life! But by using her head and coming up with a great idea, the little old lady finds that all turns out just right in the end.

FIND SOMEONE WHO . . .

1. Has walked in the woods _____

2. Has filled a basket with fruits _____

3. Can name five different pieces of clothing _____

4. Likes the fall better than any other season _____

5. Knows an older person who lives alone _____

6. Can name two uses for a scarecrow _____

7. Has worn shoes that are too big _____

8. Can name five words that rhyme with HAT _____

9. Has tried to scare someone on Halloween _____

10. Can name another story where someone walks alone through the woods and finds a small cottage _____

THE LITTLE OLD WOMAN AND THE HUNGRY CAT

by Nancy Polette; Illus. by Frank Modell, Greenwillow, 1991

A little old woman warns her cat to leave her freshly baked cupcakes alone while she goes to the mayor's house to mend his clothes. The cat eats not only the cupcakes, but a man and his pig, a groom, a bride, a best man, a maid of honor, and four horses. When the old woman returns and orders the cat out, he swallows her too, along with her sewing basket. She finds her scissors, cuts a hole in the cat's side, and all escape to have a merry wedding party while the cat spends the day sewing up the hole in his side.

FIND SOMEONE WHO . . .

1. Has put frosting on cupcakes

       _____

2. Has a cat for a pet

       _____

3. Has taken part in a wedding

       _____

4. Has petted a pig

       _____

5. Has ridden a horse

       _____

6. Had torn clothes and had to have them mended

       _____

7. Has walked along a country road

       _____

8. Can say a poem about a cat

       _____

9. Knows three words that rhyme with CAT

       _____

10. Can say a word that is the opposite of OLD

       _____

LITTLE PIERRE: A CAJUN STORY FROM LOUISIANA

by Robert D. San Souci; Illus. by David Catrow, Harcourt, 2003

Imagine the smallest of five brothers who does all the work at home helping his parents while the others do nothing. Foolish Pierre, Fat Pierre, Big Pierre, and Wise Pierre do nothing all day. A reward is offered for the person who will rescue Marie Louise, the daughter of a wealthy man from the Swamp Ogre. The brothers set off to rescue the girl and win the reward. Little Pierre follows them. Instead of rescuing the girl the brothers get themselves in big trouble. It is up to Little Pierre to save the lazy oafs as well as the young lady, proving that a sharp mind is often better than a strong arm.

FIND SOMEONE WHO. . . .

1. Is the smallest person in his or her family _____

2. Can draw a picture of an ogre _____

3. Can name two animals that live in a swamp _____

4. Can name three ways he or she helps at home _____

5. Has the first name of Marie _____

6. Is the only daughter in a family _____

7. Has visited or lived in Louisiana _____

8. Has four brothers _____

9. Has received a reward of some kind _____

10. Can make two new words using some of the letters in SWAMP _____

LON PO PO

by Ed Young, Philomel, 1989

A knock on the door is followed by the cry "Let me in, let me in it is your Lon Po Po come to visit." The three daughters who are left at home are suspicious of the visitor for they know their mother has gone to visit their grandmother. It is, of course, the wolf at the door pretending to be to be the girls' grandmother. Having the wolf come closer, clever Shang, the eldest daughter, realized it is the wolf at the door. She tempts him with ginkgo nuts, and the girls pull him in a basket to the top of the tree in which they are hiding, then let go of the rope—killing him.

FIND SOMEONE WHO . . .

1. Has two sisters

    _____

2. Has seen a real wolf

    _____

3. Has more than one grandmother

    _____

4. Can name two other stories where a wolf wants to eat some-one

    _____

5. Is the oldest child in his or her family

    _____

6. Has been at home with only brothers or sisters

    _____

7. Has climbed a tree

    _____

8. Can show the group how a wolf moves

    _____

9. Likes peanuts better than any other nut

    _____

10. Has a special name for his or her grandmother

    _____

THE LORAX

by Dr. Seuss, Random House, 1971

When the owner of a Thneeds factory chops down tree after tree; he ignores the Lorax who speaks for the trees. Not only are all the trees disappearing but there is no fruit from the trees for the starving Brown Bar-ba-loots. The factory grows bigger and bigger and emits such smelly smoke that the Swomee-Swans can't sing a note. Leftover goo from the factory machines pollutes the ponds so the Humming-Fish can no longer hum. When the last tree is cut down the factory owner and workers leave. All that was left was a bad smelling sky, an empty factory, and a barren landscape with no wildlife. Even the Lorax, who had warned of the disaster by speaking for the trees, must find another place to live.

FIND SOMEONE WHO . . .

1. Lives near a factory

   _____

2. Does not have a tree in his or her yard

   _____

3. Has watched someone cut down a tree

   _____

4. Can name two good things growing trees do

   _____

5. Can name two ways to protect the Earth from pollution

   _____

6. Can name two fruits that grow on trees

   _____

7. Can name an animal that lives in a tree

   _____

8. Can tell what happens to fish in a polluted stream

   _____

9. Knows why some wild animals are disappearing

   _____

10. Can name something made from trees

    _____

MADELINE

by Ludwig Bemelmans, Viking, 1939, Reissue 1977

Twelve little girls, including Madeline, lived together in an old house in Paris, looked after by Miss Clavel. They took daily walks in rain or shine and did everything together. Madeline wasn't afraid of anything. Not mice or ice or even the tiger in the zoo! But she did frighten Miss Clavel in the middle of the night. The doctor was called and Madeline was taken to the hospital for an operation. When she was well enough for visitors she showed everyone her scar. Guess what the other little girls all wanted!

FIND SOMEONE WHO . . .

1. Has a first name beginning with the letter M

2. Knows what an appendix is

3. Has been a patient in a hospital

4. Has seen a real tiger

5. Likes to walk in the rain

6. Has visited a sick friend

7. Can find France on a map

8. Can say "Hello" in French

9. Can name 12 different girls

10. Can name two words that rhyme with FRANCE

MADELINE'S RESCUE

by Ludwig Bemelmans, Viking, 1953

The smallest of 12 little girls who lived in an old house in Paris was Madeline. She loved winter and was not afraid of anything, not even mice or tigers. Miss Clavel, who looked after the little girls, was quite frightened indeed when Madeline fell into the canal on one of their daily walks. Fortunately she was rescued by a dog who was named Genevieve and became part of the household. But when the trustees came for their annual inspection, they threw Genevieve out and ordered that no dogs be allowed in the house. The little girls are heartbroken until Genevieve returns with a family of her own.

FIND SOMEONE WHO . . .

1. Has taken a walk by a river   _____

2. Has brought a stray dog home   _____

3. Has visited or lived in a big city   _____

4. Can name four pets other than a dog   _____

5. Has dressed up in funny clothes   _____

6. Has lost a pet   _____

7. Can find the word TRUSTEE in a dictionary   _____

8. Can find Paris on a map   _____

9. Has awakened three times in one night   _____

10. Shares a bedroom with someone else   _____

MAKE WAY FOR DUCKLINGS

by Robert McCloskey, Viking, 1941

"Look out!" squawked Mrs. Mallard. "You'll get run over!" The Public Garden in Boston was a dangerous place to raise a family of ducklings, so the search began for a new home. Mr. and Mrs. Mallard flew over Beacon Hill, around the State House, through Louisburg Square, and over the Charles River to a quiet island. This would be a better place for hatching ducklings. When the time came to venture out into the world with the newly hatched ducklings, things were far from quiet! The family of ducks needed some help from special friends to protect them from real danger. It was up to Michael and the other Boston police officers to come to their rescue and make way for ducklings!

FIND SOMEONE WHO . . .

1. Can name one way a policeman helps people

   _____

2. Has seen ducks swimming in a pond

   _____

3. Can find Boston on a map

   _____

4. Has visited or lived in a big city

   _____

5. Has lived in more than one house

   _____

6. Knows the name of the crossing guard at a school

   _____

7. Has helped younger children cross a street

   _____

8. Has two brothers and two sisters

   _____

9. Has seen a newly hatched duckling or chick

   _____

10. Knows what an island is

   _____

THE MAN WHO WALKED BETWEEN THE TOWERS

by *Mordicai Gerstein,* Roaring Brook Press, 2003

In 1974 a young French aerialist had a dream to perform high in the air on a tight-rope tied to the two towers of the almost completed World Trade Center in New York City. He dressed as a construction worker and, with a friend, carried every-thing he needed up 180 stairs to the roof. For more than an hour he walked and danced on a cable between the towers. After his performance, which startled many New Yorkers watching below, he was taken to jail and brought before a judge. His punishment was to perform for children in the park.

FIND SOMEONE WHO . . .

1. Has played a trick on someone

2. Has a last name beginning with the letter P

3. Has had a wish come true

4. Can find the state of New York on a map

5. Can name a daring feat

6. Can name three sights to see in New York City

7. Can find France on a map

8. Has watched a street performer

9. Has seen a tightrope walker at a circus

10. Can name a famous park in New York City

MANY MOONS

by James Thurber; Illus. by Louis Slobodkin, Harcourt, Brace, Jovanovich, 1943

Princess Lenore lived in a palace and was dearly loved by her parents, the King and Queen. One day she became quite ill. She had eaten too many raspberry tarts. She insisted that only one thing would make her better. Someone must bring her the moon. Impossible! The moon was much too far away. What was to be done? The Court Jester found the answer to fulfilling such an impossible request by asking the princess how the moon might be obtained. You will agree she had a very sensible answer.

FIND SOMEONE WHO . . .

1. Can name another story with a princess

   _____

2. Can draw a picture of a full moon

   _____

3. Knows what color a raspberry is

   _____

4. Has a first name that begins with the letter L

   _____

5. Can make two new words using some of the letters in PALACE

   _____

6. Has become ill after eating too much candy

   _____

7. Can name two things in the sky other than the moon

   _____

8. Knows another word that means the same as KING

   _____

9. Knows what a Court Jester does

   _____

10. Can draw a picture of a palace

    _____

MAY I BRING A FRIEND?

by Beatrice de Regniers; Illus. by Beni Montresor, Atheneum, 1971

The King and Queen are most gracious hosts to a certain little boy—and any friend of his is a friend of theirs. When he brings a giraffe to tea, the King doesn't blink an eye and says, "Hello. How do you do?" and the Queen merely exclaims, "Well! Fancy meeting you!" The royal pair continue to invite the boy as their guest for tea, breakfast, lunch, dinner, apple pie, and Halloween, and each time he politely asks if he can bring a friend, waits for their assent, then brings a hippo, monkeys, an elephant, and once even a pride of lions into their elegant home. Of course, animals in a palace are sure to cause some damage even if they are well behaved but the polite King and Queen don't seem to mind at all.

FIND SOMEONE WHO . . .

1. Likes pancakes as his or her favorite breakfast

   _____

2. Can name another story with a king or queen

   _____

3. Has dressed as a princess on Halloween

   _____

4. Has taken a friend (who was not invited) to a party

   _____

5. Has seen a real hippo

   _____

6. Can draw a picture of an elephant

   _____

7. Likes apple pie best for dessert

   _____

8. Can name one place you could find a giraffe

   _____

9. Can name polite words to say

   _____

10. Can name two vegetables often found on a dinner plate

    _____

MEI LI

by Thomas Handforth, Doubleday, 1938

Mei Li was busy helping her mother prepare for the visit of the kitchen god who would come at midnight on New Year's Eve. When Mei Li heard her brother talk about going to the fair in the city, she was sad because little girls had to stay at home. However, with her three lucky pennies and her three lucky marbles, she tagged along with her brother to the fair knowing she must return home before midnight to greet the kitchen god. Arriving home just in time she learns that her home is her kingdom and in this palace all living things are her subjects.

FIND SOMEONE WHO . . .

1. Can find China on a map _____

2. Has a first name that begins with the letter M _____

3. Has stayed up until midnight _____

4. Knows the date of New Year's Day each year _____

5. Has visited a fair _____

6. Has an older brother _____

7. Knows another story where someone must be home by midnight _____

8. Has played a game of marbles _____

9. Can name something to buy with three pennies _____

10. Lives in or has visited a large city _____

MICE TWICE

by Joseph Low, Aladdin, 1986

Suppose you were a mouse and a hungry cat invited you to dinner. Would you accept the invitation? A small mouse does say yes but asks if she can bring a friend. The cat assumes that a mouse's friend would be another mouse and says the friend will be welcome. The hungry cat who expects to eat two mice rather than one is fooled when the friend turns out to be a dog. When the supper is over the dog asks the cat if he will come the next night for supper. The cat says yes but asks if he may also bring a friend that turns out to be a wolf. Bigger and bigger animals join cat and mouse for their suppers with an ending that will surprise the reader.

FIND SOMEONE WHO . . .

1. Has had dinner at another person's house

   _____

2. Has invited someone to dinner

   _____

3. Can name another story with a cat

   _____

4. Can say a nursery rhyme about a mouse

   _____

5. Can name two words that rhyme with DOG

   _____

6. Can name another story with a wolf

   _____

7. Can name an animal bigger than a wolf

   _____

8. Likes hamburgers best for supper

   _____

9. Has a friend whose first name begins with the letter D or M

   _____

10. Can draw a picture of a mouse

    _____

MIKE MULLIGAN AND HIS STEAM SHOVEL

by Virginia Lee Burton, Houghton Mifflin, 1967

Mike Mulligan and his steam shovel, Mary Anne, had worked together for many years. They dug canals, tunnels, and roadways. Mike bragged that Mary Anne could dig as much in a day as 100 men could dig in a week. The two are put to the test and asked to dig a basement for the Town Hall. Mike and Mary Anne are so busy digging that they forget to plan how to get out of the large hole. Then a young boy thinks of a perfect solution. Mary Anne will be needed for years to come!

FIND SOMEONE WHO . . .

1. Can name something a steam shovel can do

   _____

2. Has thrown thrown away something old

   _____

3. Can name a good friend

   _____

4. Can give five reasons to dig a hole

   _____

5. Has made a promise and kept it

   _____

6. Can tell what a Town Hall is for

   _____

7. Lives or has lived in a small town

   _____

8. Knows someone named Mary

   _____

9. Knows what OBSOLETE means

   _____

10. Knows someone named Mike

   _____

MILLIONS OF CATS

by Wanda Gag, Coward-MacCann, 1928

A little old man and a little old woman were lonely so they decided that a cat was just what they needed for company. The little old man set out to find a cat, walking through cool valleys until he came to a hill covered with cats. There were hundreds of cats, thousands of cats, millions and billions and trillions of cats and every single one of them followed him home. Now the old couple knew they could not not possibly feed all of the cats so they let the cats decide which one was the prettiest and that is the one they would keep. But the little old man and the little old woman are in for quite a surprise when they see what happens. You will be surprised, too, when you read *Millions of Cats*.

FIND SOMEONE WHO . . .

1. Knows an older couple with a cat _____

2. Has climbed a hill _____

3. Has seen more than three cats together _____

4. Can name another story about a cat _____

5. Has heard two or more cats fight _____

6. Has had an animal follow him or her home _____

7. Has visited or lived in the country _____

8. Can write the number one million _____

9. Can say five words that rhyme with CAT _____

10. Can name three members of the cat family _____

MING LO MOVES THE MOUNTAIN

by Arnold Lobel, Greenwillow, 1982

Many years ago Ming Lo and his wife lived in a house near a large mountain. Rocks falling from the mountain damaged their house. The mountain also kept their crops from growing. Determined to get rid of their problem, the wife begs Ming Lo to do away with the mountain. Ming Lo goes to the wise man in the village for advice. The wise man makes many suggestions to solve the problem. Ming Lo and his wife try and try and try but the mountain does not go away. Ming Lo returns to the wise man for the fourth time to seek advice. He tells Ming Lo and his wife how to take care of the mountain once and for all. Will Ming Lo and his wife live in peace? Will the mountain be moved? To find out, read *Ming Lo Moves the Mountain*.

FIND SOMEONE WHO . . .

1. Has climbed a mountain   _____

2. Can say a word that rhymes with MING   _____

3. Has planted something good to eat   _____

4. Can name three crops farmers grow   _____

5. Can give the name of one mountain   _____

6. Can find China on a map   _____

7. Likes carrots better than any other vegetable   _____

8. Is good at solving math problems   _____

9. Has a rock collection   _____

10. Has skipped a rock in a stream or lake   _____

MINTY: A STORY OF YOUNG HARRIET TUBMAN

by Alan Schroeder; Illus. by Jerry Pinkney, Dial, 1996

Young Harriet Tubman was stubborn and headstrong. She refused to listen to older, wiser heads and was considered a problem slave by her master. She lived on the Brodas plantation in the 1820s and was more often in trouble than not. At one time she suffered a severe blow on the head. Here is the story of a child who told Bible stories to her torn rag doll, who was sometimes too bold for her own good, and who learned from her father three survival skills: how to follow the North Star, how to skin a squirrel, and how to read a tree, all things that would one day help her to escape to freedom.

FIND SOMEONE WHO . . .

1. Can name a stubborn character in a book

2. Has the first name of Harriet or knows someone with the first name of Harriet

3. Knows what a plantation is

4. Has had a hard bump on the head

5. Has a favorite doll

6. Can draw a picture of the North Star

7. Can give two names found in the Bible

8. Has squirrels in his or her back yard

9. Has climbed a tree

10. Has had a time-out for misbehaving

MIRANDY AND BROTHER WIND

by Patricia C. McKissack; Illus. by Jerry Pinkney, Knopf, 1988

"Whoever catch the Wind can make him do their bidding," Ma Dear tells Mirandy who wants the wind to be her partner at the junior cakewalk. But catching the wind proves to be a formidable task. Mirandy asks Grandmama Beasley and all her neighbors how to go about capturing Brother Wind, but no one has the answer. She tries putting black pepper out and throwing a quilt on the Wind. She learns a conjure from Mis' Poinsettia and follows all the directions but finds Brother Wind just laughing at her from the other side of a tree. Finally she locks the Wind in the barn. At the cakewalk Mirandy finds the girls making fun of her friend Ezel and tells them that he is to be her partner and that there is no doubt the two of them will win that cake. And win they do, with Mirandy wearing Mis' Poinsettia's scarves and Ezel standing tall with his head high.

FIND SOMEONE WHO . . .

1. Can name two good uses for wind _____

2. Has a first name that begins with the letter M _____

3. Can name something he or she tried to catch but it got away _____

4. Has a quilt on his or her bed at home _____

5. Can perform a dance for the group _____

6. Who has a grandmother whose last name begins with the letter B _____

7. Knows what a cakewalk is _____

8. Can name something to sprinkle with black pepper _____

9. Has walked around in a barn _____

10. Has won something in a contest _____

MIRETTE ON THE HIGH WIRE

by Emily Arnold McCully, G.P. Putnam's Sons, 1992

One day, a mysterious stranger arrives at the boardinghouse of the Widow Gateau. He is a sad-faced stranger who keeps to himself. When the widow's daughter, Mirette, discovers him crossing the courtyard on air, she begs him to teach her how he does it. But Mirette doesn't know that the stranger was once the Great Bellini—master wire walker. Or that Bellini has been stopped by a terrible fear. And it is she who must teach him courage once again.

FIND SOMEONE WHO . . .

1. Has been to a circus _____

2. Is in a gymnastics class _____

3. Helps with jobs at home _____

4. Has been hurt in a fall _____

5. Can find France on a map _____

6. Knows in what state Niagara
   Falls is located _____

7. Knows where the Alps are _____

8. Knows in what country Barcelona
   is found _____

9. Has watched a high-wire act _____

10. Knows a girl whose first name
    starts with the letter M _____

MISS NELSON IS MISSING!

by Harry Allard; Illus. by James Marshall, Houghton Mifflin, 1977

The kids in Room 207 were about the worst kids in the school. They threw spitballs, were rude during story hour, and never did their homework. Their teacher, Miss Nelson, was a very kind person but even kind people don't like being taken advantage of. She stopped coming to school and her replacement was the dreaded Miss Viola Swamp. No one misbehaved in Miss Swamp's class. Everyone did homework. Not a spitball was thrown and there was NO story hour. The children went to the police for help in finding Miss Nelson but the police couldn't help. They were just about to give up hope when Miss Nelson returned. She discovered that her students had changed for the better and smiled to herself as she put away Miss Viola Swamp's clothes in her closet that night.

FIND SOMEONE WHO . . .

1. Can name a teacher whose last name starts with the letter S

   _____

2. Has been in a class that misbehaved a lot

   _____

3. Can name a word that rhymes with SWAMP

   _____

4. Likes to do homework

   _____

5. Has had a substitute teacher

   _____

6. Likes math better than any other subject

   _____

7. Has never thrown a spitball

   _____

8. Looks forward to story hour

   _____

9. Knows what a disguise is

   _____

10. Can give the name of one policeman

    _____

MISS RUMPHIUS

by Barbara Cooney, Viking, 1982

Miss Rumphius's first name was Alice and when she was small she dreamed of traveling to faraway places and living by the sea. Her grandfather told her that she must also make the world a more beautiful place in which to live. Miss Rumphius did travel to far away places and saw coconuts and cockatoos on tropical islands, lions in the grasslands, and monkeys in the jungle. On a hillside she found lupine and jasmines growing and rode a camel across the desert to meet a kangaroo in an Australian town. Yes, Miss Rumphius did almost everything she wanted to do. In her later years she even lived by the sea. That was when she did something to make the world a more beautiful place. Can you guess what it was?

FIND SOMEONE WHO . . .

1. Has lived in a city by the sea   _____

2. Has helped a grandparent do a job   _____

3. Goes to the library once a week   _____

4. Can name one thing to see on a tropical isle   _____

5. Can name something beautiful in nature   _____

6. Has seen a real camel   _____

7. Has planted flower seeds   _____

8. Can name two ways to help keep the Earth clean   _____

9. Can find Australia on a map   _____

10. Can name one of the two oceans that border the United States   _____

MISS SPIDER'S TEA PARTY

by David Kirk, Scholastic, 1994

Miss Spider was lonely. She decided to give a tea party and invite all of the insects she saw flying by. But the insects knew it was not a good thing to be caught in a spider web. They might end up being Miss Spider's dinner. She watched sadly as beetles, fireflies, bumblebees, ants, and butterflies passed her by. Miss Spider sipped her tea and cried. No one wanted to be her friend. It was then she spied a small, wet moth who had been caught in a thunderstorm. It could not fly until its wings were dry. Miss Spider lifted him up and dried him off. She gave him tea. When he was dry she tossed him gently in the air. The grateful moth told other insects that Miss Spider meant them no harm. The all came to tea and Miss Spider was never lonely again.

FIND SOMEONE WHO . . .

1. Can name someone who lives alone

   _____

2. Has invited friends to a party

   _____

3. Has brushed away a spider web

   _____

4. Has found a spider in his or her kitchen

   _____

5. Has ignored an invitation

   _____

6. Knows what GLOOMY means

   _____

7. Has gathered flowers to make a bouquet

   _____

8. Has gotten all wet in a thunder-storm

   _____

9. Can name four different insects

   _____

10. Can say three words that rhyme with BUG

   _____

THE MITTEN

by Jan Brett, G.P. Putnam's Sons, 1989

Nicki begs his grandmother, Baba, to knit him a pair of white mittens. In spite of her warnings that he will lose them and that they will be hard to find in the snow, he insists and she finally does so. Grandmothers, however, are usually right and it isn't long before he has dropped a mitten. A mole is the first to discover the mitten lying on the snow and crawls inside, followed by a snowshoe rabbit, a hedgehog, an owl, a badger, a fox, a bear, and finally a mouse. Each time the inhabitants protest that there's not enough room for the newcomer, and grandmother's knitted mitten stretches and stretches and stretches. Just at the point where Nicki approaches, searching for his lost mitten, the mouse causes the bear to sneeze and the mitten and all its occupants go flying. The boy finds the mitten and puts it on. It's who grandmother sees how stretched-out mitten is and wonders what happened to it. Only the reader knows.

FIND SOMEONE WHO . . .

1. Has a pet name for his or her grandmother _____

2. Has received a pair of knitted mittens _____

3. Has lost a mitten _____

4. Can name three animals that live in the woods _____

5. Knows where a mole is usually found _____

6. Can name a forest animal larger than a fox _____

7. Can say a nursery rhyme about lost mittens _____

8. Can draw a picture of an owl _____

9. Has made a snowman _____

10. Likes winter better than spring, summer, or fall _____

MOOSELTOE

by Margie Palatini; Illus. by Henry Cole, Hyperion, 2000

Moose is getting ready for Christmas. He wants everything perfectly perfect. He makes lists and has written everything down that needs to be done. And then he starts doing everything on his lists. He invites his family to share Christmas with him. He sends out cards, buys presents, and bakes cookies. Everything on his lists is done. Then Moose realizes he had forgotten to write "Buy Christmas tree" on his list. He sets out to find a tree on Christmas Eve with no luck at all. What is Moose to do? He stands in a corner and becomes the tree himself, letting his family hang tinsel and ornaments from his long mustache, wrap lights around his antlers, and stick a star on the top of his head.

FIND SOMEONE WHO. . . .

1. Has made a list of things to do

   _____

2. Has made a holiday card for
   someone

   _____

3. Has helped to bake cookies

   _____

4. Has had family members visit for
   a holiday

   _____

5. Has decorated a Christmas tree

   _____

6. Has put a star on top of a tree

   _____

7. Can think if a bird whose name
   rhymes with MOOSE

   _____

8. Can name three holidays other
   than Christmas

   _____

9. Can tell about a time he or she
   forgot to do something

   _____

10. Can name another book by Mar-
    gie Palatini

   _____

MOSS GOWN

by William H. Hooks; Illus. by Donald Carrick, Clarion, 1987

Her greedy stepsisters turn a young girl out into the stormy night where she is picked up by the wind and dropped into a bed of moss. A witch woman gives her a moss gown that is magical as long as the Morning Star shines. When the Star fades, the gown turns to rags. Moss Gown reaches a fine house and works doing hard chores in the kitchen. The Young Master of the house holds a ball each night. Moss Gown wears her beautiful dress and dances a with the Young Master. But she must disappear before the Morning Star rises. The Young Master searches in vain for the girl with whom he has fallen in love and falls ill because he cannot eat. Moss Gown takes him his supper and remains until the Morning Star rises. Her gown turns to rags but the Young Master sees only the beautiful and kind girl and they are married.

FIND SOMEONE WHO . . .

1. Has lived in or visited a southern state

2. Knows what color moss is

3. Can spell the word PLANTATION

4. Has two sisters

5. Lives in a white house

6. Has walked in the woods

7. Has been away from home more than one week

8. Has green eyes

9. Knows another name for the Morning Star

10. Has helped doing a job in the kitchen

MUFARO'S BEAUTIFUL DAUGHTERS

by John Steptoe, Lothrop, Lee & Shepard, 1987

Long ago in Africa, Mufaro had two beautiful daughters. Manyara was selfish and greedy and teased her sister Nyasha, who was kind and loving. Manyara spent her days in a bad temper; Nyasha spent her days tending her garden and singing to her friend, the little garden snake. The Great King is looking for a wife. Mufaro decides that both his daughters will go to appear before the king. Manyara is sure she will be chosen queen. Nyasha would prefer to remain in the village tending her garden and looking after her father. Manyara sneaks off into the night ignoring a hungry boy and an old woman's advice. Nyasha gives food to the boy and sunflower seeds to the old woman. When she reaches the city she finds her frightened sister who has seen the king and describes him as a monster snake with five heads. When Nyasha enters the chamber she finds her friend, the garden snake, who changes into the shape of the king and asks her to be his wife.

FIND SOMEONE WHO . . .

1. Can find Africa on a map

   _____

2. Has helped someone tend a garden

   _____

3. Has held a harmless snake in his or her hand

   _____

4. Lives or has lived in a small town or village

   _____

5. Can name another story with a king

   _____

6. Has taken the advice of an older person

   _____

7. Can describe a selfish act

   _____

8. Can describe an act of kindness

   _____

9. Has visited or lives in a big city

   _____

10. Can name a word that is the opposite of SELFISH

    _____

MY FRIEND RABBIT

by Eric Rohmann, Roaring Brook Press, 2002

When Mouse lets his best friend, Rabbit, play with his brand new airplane, Rabbit tries to launch the plane but it ends up in a tree, too high to reach. Rabbit has an idea. He gathers together many animals and gets them to climb on each other. A tall tree of animals results with rhino on top of elephant, hippo on top of rhino, antelope on top of hippo, crocodile on top of antelope, bear on top of crocodile, goose on top of bear, and squirrel on top of goose holding Mouse. Reaching for the plane proves to be a disaster when the animal ladder collapses. Mouse is left hanging onto the wing of the plane that is still stuck in the tree. Finally the plane is rescued but trouble looms again when Rabbit tries to take a plane ride with Mouse.

FIND SOMEONE WHO . . .

1. Has broken a toy $\rule{8cm}{0.4pt}$

2. Has a toy airplane at home $\rule{8cm}{0.4pt}$

3. Has tried to reach something that was too high $\rule{8cm}{0.4pt}$

4. Has loaned a toy to a good friend $\rule{8cm}{0.4pt}$

5. Has seen a rabbit in a yard $\rule{8cm}{0.4pt}$

6. Has climbed on someone's shoulders $\rule{8cm}{0.4pt}$

7. Has seen a real hippo $\rule{8cm}{0.4pt}$

8. Can say a word that rhymes with RABBIT $\rule{8cm}{0.4pt}$

9. Has a tall tree in his or her yard $\rule{8cm}{0.4pt}$

10. Has had a kite caught in a tree $\rule{8cm}{0.4pt}$

MY GREAT-AUNT ARIZONA

by Gloria Houston; Illus. by Susan Condie Lamb, HarperCollins, 1992

Arizona was born in a log cabin her papa built. She grew into a tall girl who liked to sing, square-dance, and—most of all—read and dream of the faraway places she would visit one day. Arizona never did make it to those places. Instead she became a teacher, helping generations of children in the one-room schoolhouse that she herself had attended. When Arizona married and had a daughter, the baby went to school with her. For 57 years Arizona taught not only reading, writing, and arithmetic, but how to make dreams come true even if they aren't exactly the dreams one started with.

FIND SOMEONE WHO . . .

1. Has seen a one-room schoolhouse   _____

2. Has been inside a log cabin   _____

3. Is the tallest person in the class   _____

4. Has caught tadpoles in a creek   _____

5. Has taken his or her lunch to
   school   _____

6. Has walked to school in the snow   _____

7. Likes reading better than any
   other subject   _____

8. Has lived in another state   _____

9. Has visited or lived in another
   country   _____

10. Can find Arizona on a map   _____

THE NAPPING HOUSE

by Audrey Wood; Illus. by Don Wood, Harcourt, 1984

This gentle story is about a snoring granny, a dreaming child, a dozing dog, a snoozing cat, and a slumbering mouse, all on one cozy bed. But wait! When a wakeful flea arrives to join the rest there is a surprise in store and no one is sleeping anymore. Imagine all of the sleepers tumbling off the bed on to the floor. Now everyone is awake in the Napping House.

FIND SOMEONE WHO . . .

1. Has a dog for a pet _____

2. Has more than one cat at home _____

3. Has the color blue somewhere on his or her house _____

4. Has more than one grandmother _____

5. Has found a mouse in his or her house _____

6. Has been awakened by an animal _____

7. Likes to go to bed early _____

8. Has fallen out of bed _____

9. Can name a word that rhymes with MOUSE _____

10. Can name two words that rhyme with FLEA _____

NO, DAVID!

by David Shannon, Blue Sky Press, 1998

David is not your ideal, well behaved child. He colors on the walls, tracks mud all over the rug, and jumps on the bed without taking his boots off. At the same time he hears "Come back here!" "Be quiet!" "Not in the house, David!" and "No!" David picks his nose, runs down the street bare-bottomed, and breaks his mother's vase with a baseball. Yet, despite all his misbehavior, David's mother puts her arms around him and says, "Yes, David, I love you."

FIND SOMEONE WHO . . .

1. Has tracked mud in the house

    _____

2. Has jumped on a bed

    _____

3. Has colored on a wall

    _____

4. Has a little brother who sometimes misbehaves

    _____

5. Has been told "NO" by an adult

    _____

6. Has the first name of David

    _____

7. Has been hugged today by a family member

    _____

8. Can be very quiet for a long time

    _____

9. Can name something he or she
   was told not to do in the house

    _____

10. Has broken something that be-
    longed to someone else

    _____

OFFICER BUCKLE AND GLORIA

by Peggy Rathmann, G.P. Putnam's Sons, 1995

Officer Buckle knows more about safety than anyone in the town of Napville. But whenever he tries to share his safety tips, nobody listens. Until, that is, the Napville Police Department buys a police dog named Gloria. Unbeknownst to Officer Buckle, Gloria has her own way of demonstrating safety tips—one that makes Napville sit up and take notice. Suddenly, everybody wants to hear Officer Buckle's safety speech. "And please," the people say, "bring along the police dog." When Office Buckle discovers he's been upstaged, he vows to give up safety tips once and for all. Can Gloria convince her friend to return to the job he loves, or is Napville about to have its worst accident ever?

FIND SOMEONE WHO . . .

1. Can give a safety tip to the class _____

2. Has a brown dog for a pet _____

3. Has a relative who is a policeman _____

4. Knows what K-9 means _____

5. Has written a thank-you letter _____

6. Knows what ENORMOUS means _____

7. Knows someone named Gloria _____

8. Can name three duties of a policeman _____

9. Can say a word that rhymes with BUCKLE _____

10. Has spilled a glass of milk _____

THE OLD LADIES WHO LIKED CATS

by Carol Greene; Illus. by Loretta Krupinski, HarperCollins, 1991;
Harper Trophy Reprint 1994

ALL CATS MUST BE LOCKED UP! Once there was a town on a beautiful island—an island kept safe by a unique ecological chain made up of cows, clover, bees, mice, cats, and the old ladies who liked them. But then, when the mayor trips over a cat, he decides that all cats must be locked up at night. Now the delicate balance of nature is disturbed, and the island is no longer secure. Pirates come ashore on the island and want to make all the rules. Can the old ladies who liked cats set things right again?

FIND SOMEONE WHO . . .

1. Has more than one cat at home _____

2. Has watched someone milk a cow _____

3. Has found a four-leaf clover _____

4. Has found a mouse in the house _____

5. Can name a story with a pirate _____

6. Can name the mayor of your city
   or town _____

7. Knows what an island is _____

8. Can name one good thing about
   bees _____

9. Can say three words that rhyme
   with CAT _____

10. Has kept a pet indoors at night _____

OLIVIA

by Ian Falconer, Simon & Schuster, 2000

Olivia's mother is exhausted after keeping up with her active and imaginative daughter. One of the things Olivia is best at is wearing people out including herself. Olivia gets annoyed when her little brother, Ian, copies everything that she does, but she does lead an interesting life! It is hard to decide what to wear each day so she tries on everything. Her sand castles at the beach are amazing and who has time for a nap when there is so much to do? Olivia loves visiting museums where she has a favorite painting and creates similar art on a wall at home, much to the dismay of her mother. But Olivia's favorite activity is the bedtime story with her mother and mother, who loves her active daughter immensely, is ready for bed too.

FIND SOMEONE WHO . . .

1. Can do one thing better than anything else

   _____

2. Has more than one little brother

   _____

3. Takes care of a pet

   _____

4. Sometimes can't choose what to wear

   _____

5. Has stayed in the sun too long

   _____

6. Does not like to take a map

   _____

7. Has visited a museum

   _____

8. Has drawn a picture on a wall

   _____

9. Has made a sand castle at the beach

   _____

10. Can name a favorite bedtime story

    _____

ON MARKET STREET

by Arnold Lobel; Illus. by Anita Lobel, Greenwillow, 1981

In this alphabet book each shopkeeper is composed of his or her wares. As we visit shop after another we see apples (food for the body), books (food for the mind), clocks, doughnuts, eggs—the list goes on with each seller more elaborate than the last.

FIND SOMEONE WHO . . .

1. Has gone shopping with a parent _____

2. Can name three different kinds of shops _____

3. Can name four foods that begin with the first four letters of the alphabet _____

4. Has visited a clock shop _____

5. Can name a favorite book _____

6. Likes scrambled eggs better than any other kind _____

7. Can name something beginning with the letter M you would find on Market Street _____

8. Does not like to go shopping _____

9. Has gone shopping alone _____

10. Can say two words that rhyme with STREET _____

ONCE A MOUSE

by Marcia Brown, Simon & Schuster, 1961

An old hermit magician made a tiger from a mouse. The hermit befriended the frightened little mouse. When a cat attempted to attack the mouse, the hermit turned the mouse into a stout cat, then into a big dog, and finally into a proud and royal tiger. But the royal tiger became too proud and forgot how he became a tiger. He plotted against the hermit who tried to remind the tiger of his humble beginnings. The hermit read the tiger's mind and again used his magic to turn the tiger into a frightened, humble little mouse. Then the hermit sat thinking about big and little.

FIND SOMEONE WHO . . .

1. Knows what a hermit is _____

2. Can do a magic trick for the group _____

3. Can name a creature smaller than a mouse _____

4. Can name a creature larger than a tiger _____

5. Has a friend whose last name begins with the letter M _____

6. Can say a word that rhymes with MOUSE _____

7. Knows in what country tigers are found _____

8. Can name another member of the cat family _____

9. Knows what HUMBLE means _____

10. Knows what STOUT means _____

ONE FINE DAY

by Nonny Hogrogian, Simon & Schuster, 1971

A fox laps up all the milk in an old woman's pail and she is so angry that she cuts his tail off. The fox begs for the old woman to sew his tail back on. Otherwise, "all my friends will laugh at me." The old woman tells the fox that he can have his tail if he gives her back her milk The fox finds a cow who is willing to help, but wants grass in return. The fox asks a field for some grass, and the field asks for some water. The fox goes to the stream, which tells him to get a jug for the water. From there, the fox finds a fair maiden who has a jug but wants a blue bead. The fox finds a peddler who has a blue bead but wants an egg. An hen offers an egg in exchange for some grain. The fox finds a miller who gives him grain. In the end, the old woman carefully sewed his tail in place, and off he ran to join his friends.

FIND SOMEONE WHO . . .

1. Has spilled a glass of milk

   _____

2. Has seen a real fox

   _____

3. Knows what a cow eats

   _____

4. Knows what grass needs in order
   to grow

   _____

5. Has a necklace with blue beads

   _____

6. Can name three ways to cook
   eggs

   _____

7. Knows what a miller does

   _____

8. Has sewed a button on a shirt or
   blouse

   _____

9. Can name three animals found on
   a farm

   _____

10. Can name another word that
    means the same as PAIL

    _____

OWEN

by Kevin Henkes, Greenwillow, 1993

On the day before his first day in kindergarten, Owen is still holding on to his baby blanket that he has named Fuzzy. A neighbor, Mrs. Tweezers, says to Owen's parents that she thinks Owen is much too old to be carrying around an old fuzzy blanket. She offers free advice as to how to get rid of it such as dipping the blanket in vinegar or stealing it away at night. While Owen's mother agrees that the blanket should go, she comes up with a much better solution. With her needle and thread she turns the blanket into a stack of very usable handkerchiefs. Not only does this make Owen happy but it stops Mrs. Tweezers from offering more suggestions.

FIND SOMEONE WHO . . .

1. Had a favorite blanket as a young child

2. Has a first name that begins with the letter O

3. Missed the first day of kindergarten

4. Has a neighbor whose last name begins with the letter T

5. Has had the same favorite toy for more than two years

6. Is in a class with more boys than girls

7. Can say a nursery rhyme about a mouse

8. Can sing a happy song

9. Can show the group a game learned in kindergarten

10. Has a handkerchief in his or her pocket

OWL MOON

by Jane Yolen; Illus. by John Schoenherr, Philomel, 1987

A little girl is excited when her father takes her into the woods on a snowy night to see the Great Horned Owl. The two quietly make their way among the tall trees, calling to the owl. To their delight the owl answers. This is a gentle tale of the warm relationship between father and daughter and their discoveries of the many beautiful things to be found in nature.

FIND SOMEONE WHO . . .

1. Knows what it means to go owl-ing

    _____

2. Can name three things to do in the snow

    _____

3. Has seen a real owl

    _____

4. Has walked in the woods at night

    _____

5. Can draw a picture of a full moon

    _____

6. Has taken a walk with an older person

    _____

7. Can name a word that rhymes with MOON

    _____

8. Likes to play in the snow

    _____

9. Can name two beautiful things found in nature

    _____

10. Can change one letter in TREE to make a new word

    _____

OX-CART MAN

by Donald Hall; Illus. by Barbara Cooney, Viking, 1979

In October the father of a farm family loads his ox cart with things the family has grown or made throughout the year. He arrives in town to see all his goods: a bag of wool, a shawl his wife made, five pairs of mittens, candles, linen, shingles, birch brooms, honey, vegetables, maple sugar, and goose feathers. Nothing on the farm is wasted. Something is used for every purpose. He sells all of his goods, including the ox and buys an iron kettle, a needle, a knife, and peppermint candies. When he arrives home with his gifts, the year begins again with the family growing or making all of the goods to be sold at next year's market.

FIND SOMEONE WHO . . .

1. Has visited or lived on a farm _____

2. Has made something to sell _____

3. Can tell what to do with a shawl _____

4. Has more than one pair of mittens _____

5. Likes honey on biscuits _____

6. Knows where maple syrup comes from _____

7. Can name one use for goose feathers _____

8. Likes peppermint candies _____

9. Has been to a farmer's market _____

10. Likes corn better than any other vegetable _____

THE PAPERBOY

by Dav Pilkey, Orchard Books, 1996

A paperboy and his dog rouse themselves on a cold morning, eat breakfast from bowls, prepare the newspapers, and set off on their paper route. They travel together along the still moonlit route delivering papers until they see the brilliant orange sunrise. They return home just as the parents and sister are getting up and the boy and his dog crawl back into bed after pulling the shade to block out the bright sun.

FIND SOMEONE WHO . . .

1. Has a dog for a pet _____

2. Likes cereal for breakfast _____

3. Knows someone who delivers papers _____

4. Has a morning paper delivered to his or her house _____

5. Has walked around town with his or her dog _____

6. Has only one sister _____

7. Has shades rather than blinds in his or her house _____

8. Can name his or her favorite part of the newspaper _____

9. Has been out of bed before the sunrise _____

10. Can draw a picture of a new moon _____

PECOS BILL

by Steven Kellogg, Mulberry Books, 1986

Raised by coyotes, Pecos Bill grew up to be the greatest cowboy in Texas or anywhere else. Besides inventing lassoing, cattle roping, and rodeos, he could tame rattlesnakes, wrestle dangerous critters, and even make the terrible Hell's Gulch Gang turn respectable. But his two greatest feats were winning the hearts of Lightning and of Slewfoot Sue, the wildest horse and the wildest woman of the West.

FIND SOMEONE WHO . . .

1. Has lived in or visited Texas _____

2. Has watched a cattle roping contest _____

3. Has gone fishing _____

4. Has ridden a horse _____

5. Knows what sound a coyote makes _____

6. Can name five states of the United States _____

7. Has waded in a stream _____

8. Has seen a real rattlesnake _____

9. Has seen a tornado on film _____

10. Can find the Arctic Circle on a map _____

PEPPE THE LAMPLIGHTER

by Elisa Bartone; Illus. by Ted Lewin, HarperCollins, 1993

The time is the early 1900s. The place is Little Italy, where many Italian immigrants have settled in New York City. Peppe's family is very poor. His mother is dead and the boy lives with his eight sisters and his bad-tempered father who is ill and cannot work. Peppe is offered a job by the street lamplighter and is excited about being able to earn money for the family. Peppe's father disapproves of his son's new job just as he disapproves of most things. Peppe loves the work and makes a wish for those he loves with each lamp he lights. Finally, because of his father's opposition, Peppe gives up the job. Then one night his youngest sister does not come home because she is afraid of the dark. Peppe's father then pleads with him to light the lamps, admitting it is an important job.

FIND SOMEONE WHO . . .

1. Knows what an immigrant is

2. Has more than four brothers and sisters

3. Can find New York City on a map

4. Can speak a language other than English

5. Has been paid to do a job

6. Has made a wish on a star

7. Has a little sister who is afraid of the dark

8. Has a kerosene lamp at home

9. Can name something that gives light if the lights go out

10. Can name three important jobs

PETROUCHKA

by Elizabeth Cleaver, Adapted from Igor Stravinsky and Alexandre Benois, Atheneum, 1980

Petrouchka is a puppet who falls in love with a ballerina and tries but fails to win her. He dies but his spirit lives on in a freedom he had never known before. The story setting is a fair with excited children, gingerbread cookies, and a puppet theatre. At the fair Petrouchka loses his life in a fight over the dancer. As the puppet master approaches the dead puppet a wild shriek comes from the sky. On the roof of the theatre was the spirit of Petrouchka, free at last.

FIND SOMEONE WHO . . .

1. Has seen a puppet show

   _____

2. Is taking ballet lessons

   _____

3. Can perform a dance for the group

   _____

4. Has a first name that begins with the letter P

   _____

5. Likes gingerbread cookies

   _____

6. Can name a story about a gingerbread cookie

   _____

7. Has been to a fair

   _____

8. Can name another story about a puppet

   _____

9. Has dressed as a ballerina on Halloween

   _____

10. Can name three words that rhyme with FAIR

    _____

PIGGIE PIE!

by Margie Palatini; Illus. by Howard Fine, Clarion, 1995

Gritch, the witch, is hungry for something special. Her usual diet of mouse-tail stew and boiled black buzzard feet just won't do. She decides she must have Piggie Pie! She has all the ingredients she needs to make it except for eight plump piggies. Off she goes to Old Macdonald's farm only to find the pigs are missing and none of the other animals will tell her where they are. Finally she meets the farmer who tells her, "No piggies!" She threatens him with her most evil spells but he will not tell her where the piggies are. She is feeling quite discouraged when wolf comes out of the woods and tells her to forget about the pigs. "Pigs," he says, "are very tricky animals." Gritch pinches the wolf's arm and grins. She invites him home for lunch. "I've always enjoyed having a wolf for lunch," she says.

FIND SOMEONE WHO . . .

1. Can name a story with a witch _____

2. Likes pie better than cake _____

3. Can say two words that rhyme with PIG _____

4. Has helped someone make a pie _____

5. Has lived on or visited a farm _____

6. Can name four farm animals _____

7. Can sing the first two lines of "Old Macdonald" _____

8. Can name a story with a wolf _____

9. Can say five words that begin with the letter P _____

10. Can name a story with more than one pig _____

PINK AND SAY

by Patricia Polacco, Philomel, 1994

Sheldon Russell Curtis, or Say, was wounded in a fierce battle and left for dead in a pasture when Pinkus found him. He picked him up and brought him to where the black soldier's mother, Moe Moe Bay, lived. She had soft gentle hands and cared for Sheldon as well as caring for Pink, her son. But the two boys were putting Moe Moe in danger, two Union soldiers in Confederate territory! They had to get back to their outfits. Then the Confederate troops rode in. Moe Moe hid the boys in the root cellar. Her belief that the troops would not harm an old black woman was ill founded. She was shot and killed before the troops rode off. As the boys tried to make their way back to Union lines they were captured by Confederates and taken to a prison from which few emerged alive. Eventually Say is released but Pinkus dies in prison.

FIND SOMEONE WHO . . .

1. Has a last name beginning with the letter C

   _____

2. Can name a southern state

   _____

3. Can find Georgia on a map

   _____

4. Has injured his or her leg

   _____

5. Needs spectacles to read

   _____

6. Has helped someone who was hurt

   _____

7. Has washed clothes in a river or stream

   _____

8. Knows what a marauder is

   _____

9. Can recite a poem

   _____

10. Likes chicken better than any other meat

    _____

THE PIRATE'S EYE

by Robert Priest, Houghton Mifflin, 2005

Captain Black, the pirate, was having a friendly skirmish with another ship when something awful happened! His glass eye fell out! Can you imagine?? He thought it was on the ship somewhere but when the ship got to port, it rolled away. Person after person had the glass eye without knowing what it was. One morning a poor man picked up a round object in the road and took it home. That night he held the object to his eye and saw scenes from a pirate's life. He drew pictures of what he saw and made a book with the pirate's picture on the cover. The grocer put the book in his window and Captain Black saw it there. He found the poor man who gave him back his eye. When he popped it in place the images he saw were those of the hunger and hardship and generosity and kindness of the poor man's life. Captain Black felt ashamed of his pirate life and now sails the seas as a friendly merchant seaman.

FIND SOMEONE WHO . . .

1. Has been in a boat on the ocean _____

2. Can name a famous pirate _____

3. Knows what color a pirate's flag is _____

4. Has found a shiny object in the road _____

5. Has written a story about a pirate _____

6. Has lost something that was found by another person _____

7. Can draw a picture of a pirate ship _____

8. Has dressed as a pirate on Halloween _____

9. Can name three words that rhyme with SHIP _____

10. Knows what SKIRMISH means _____

THE POLAR EXPRESS

by Chris Van Allsburg, Houghton Mifflin, 1985

Late on Christmas Eve, after the town has gone to sleep, a boy boards the mysterious train that waits for him: the Polar Express, bound for the North Pole. When the boy arrives, Santa offers him any gift he desires. The boy modestly asks for one bell from the harness of the reindeer. The gift is granted. On the way home he loses the bell, but on Christmas morning he finds it under the tree. When he shakes it, the bell makes the most beautiful sound he has ever heard. His mother admires the bell but laments that it is broken, for you see, only true believers can hear the sound.

FIND SOMEONE WHO . . .

1. Has had trouble going to sleep at least once

    _____

2. Has ridden on a train

    _____

3. Has seen a real train

    _____

4. Knows what a conductor is

    _____

5. Likes hot cocoa

    _____

6. Has seen a real wolf

    _____

7. Can give the name of a mountain

    _____

8. Can find the North Pole on a map

    _____

9. Can tell what color sleigh bells are

    _____

10. Knows what a harness is

    _____
.

PUSS IN BOOTS

by Charles Perrault, Illus. by Fred Marcellino, Farrar, Straus & Giroux, 1990

When a poor miller dies his youngest son is left with nothing but a cat. The unhappy boy decides that if he gets hungry enough he can eat the cat. If he gets cold, he can make a fur muff from the cat's fur. The cat, however, has other ideas. He puts on tall boots and tells passers-by that his master, the Marquis of Carabas, is drowning. The lad is rescued and given fine clothes. Before long he obtains fields of wheat and steals a castle from an ogre. In the end, the now rich young man wins the hand of the king's daughter, all thanks to the enterprising cat.

FIND SOMEONE WHO . . .

1. Can name a fairy tale with a cat _____

2. Has more than one cat at home _____

3. Is wearing boots _____

4. Has gone swimming in a pond _____

5. Knows what food is made from wheat _____

6. Knows what an ogre is _____

7. Knows what to call a king's daughter _____

8. Has taken a stray animal home _____

9. Can name four words that rhyme with CAT _____

10. Can name another word that means SMART _____

THE RAINBOW FISH

by Marcus Pfister, North-South Books, 1992

Rainbow Fish had no equal in the ocean for beauty. He is talked about and greatly admired by all the other sea creatures, for his scales sparkle and shine with many colors—purple, green, silver, and blue. The more he was admired, the prouder he felt. Then came a day when a very small blue fish asked Rainbow Fish for one of his scales. Of course, he refused. The loss of even one scale might mar his extraordinary beauty. The blue fish was upset because Rainbow Fish would not share and he told all the other ocean creatures. It wasn't long before Rainbow Fish had no one to play with. Everyone ignored him. When he asked the octopus what he should do, the octopus told him that unless he shared his scales he was doomed to a life of loneliness. Do you think Rainbow Fish will choose beauty or the companionship of the other ocean creatures?

FIND SOMEONE WHO . . .

1. Has caught a fish _____

2. Has visited or lived near the ocean _____

3. Can name two creatures that live in the ocean _____

4. Has given someone a gift _____

5. Has shared something with a friend _____

6. Can say a word that begins with the same letter that begins OCTOPUS _____

7. Can name four colors in the rainbow _____

8. Can name two beautiful things in nature _____

9. Can name two kinds of scales _____

10. Knows what COMPANIONSHIP means _____

RAPUNZEL

by Paul O. Zelinsky, Dutton, 1997

A woman wanted some rampion that grew in the garden of a sorceress. Her husband tried to get some for her but was discovered by the witch who made him promise to give her their first-born child. The child, named Rapunzel, was imprisoned in a tall tower by the witch who visited the girl by climbing up her hair that fell like a waterfall down the side of the tower. There she remained until rescued by a prince who climbed to the top of the tower after she let down her hair.

FIND SOMEONE WHO . . .

1. Has a first name that begins with the letter R

   _____

2. Knows what rampion is

   _____

3. Can name two tales with a witch

   _____

4. Knows what a king's son is called

   _____

5. Has hair that falls below her shoulders

   _____

6. Can name a word that rhymes with TOWER

   _____

7. Has seen a real waterfall

   _____

8. Has climbed to the top of a fire tower

   _____

9. Has a water tower near his or her house

   _____

10. Has picked flowers in someone else's garden

    _____

RAVEN: A TRICKSTER TALE FROM THE PACIFIC NORTHWEST

by Gerald McDermott, Harcourt, 1993

Raven is unhappy that the world is so cold and dark. He sets off to arrive at the home of the Sky Chief and is able to transform himself into the son of the Sky Chief's daughter. Raven becomes a spoiled and demanding child and is given the shiny ball that the gods have hidden away. He transforms himself once again into a raven and escapes, bringing the shiny ball that is the sun with him. He throws the sun up into the sky where it brings light and warmth to all the people.

FIND SOMEONE WHO . . .

1. Knows what color a raven is _____

2. Can name three helpful things the sun does _____

3. Can tell one thing that would happen if the sun did not shine _____

4. Can name a place in the world where the sun does not shine for half of the year _____

5. Can name a state on the Pacific coast _____

6. Can name another story with a god or goddess _____

7. Can say a sentence with every word beginning with the letter R _____

8. Knows a word that means the same as the word TRANSFORM _____

9. Has played a trick on someone _____

10. Likes night better than day _____

RED RIDING HOOD

by James Marshall, Dial, 1991

James Marshall gives a humorous twist to the ending of this familiar tale of the little girl who takes a basket of goodies to her grandmother's house. On the way she meets a sly wolf who talks her into picking flowers while he makes his way to Granny's. Granny is more disturbed about having her reading interrupted than she is at seeing a wolf in her cottage. When Red Riding Hood arrives, Granny is nowhere to be seen. The wolf is in Granny's bed just waiting to have the little girl for dessert. The hunter saves the day and Red Riding Hood remembers that it is not wise to talk to strangers.

FIND SOMEONE WHO . . .

1. Has a red coat _____

2. Has taken a gift to a grandmother _____

3. Has helped mother bake cookies _____

4. Knows what DISGUISE means _____

5. Has walked in the woods alone _____

6. Knows what ENORMOUS means _____

7. Can spell COTTAGE correctly _____

8. Can name two kinds of trees _____

9. Can name another story with a
   wolf _____

10. Can say a word that rhymes with
    STRANGER _____

THE RELATIVES CAME

by Cynthia Rylant; Illus. by Stephen Gammell, Bradbury, 1993

In a celebration of family life, the author tells of a visit of family members from Virginia who make a yearly visit. Aunts, uncles, and cousins spend their days fixing broken things, hugging each other, playing music, eating, and relaxing. The days are full of activity with everyone pitching in when a task needs doing. Both the pictures and the text show the importance of an extended family and the joy that such a family gathering can bring.

FIND SOMEONE WHO . . .

1. Has taken a long trip in a car

_____

2. Has had relatives come to visit

_____

3. Has helped fix something that was broken

_____

4. Can play a musical instrument

_____

5. Can sing one verse of a song

_____

6. Likes fried chicken better than any other meat

_____

7. Has had a picture taken with grandparents

_____

8. Has attended a family reunion

_____

9. Knows what RELAXING means

_____

10. Has three or more aunts or uncles

_____

SAINT GEORGE AND THE DRAGON

by Margaret Hodges; Illus. by Trina Schart Hyman,
Little Brown, 1984

The Red Cross Knight has been asked by the Princess Una to fight a terrible dragon. In the battle against the ferocious foe, the Red Cross Knight falls again and again only to arise each time to attack anew. At last, the dragon is slain. The Knight marries Princess Una but gives his gifts of riches to the poor, thus becoming known as Saint George.

FIND SOMEONE WHO . . .

1. Knows the name of a real dragon living today

   _____

2. Can sing a song about a dragon

   _____

3. Knows what the daughter of a king is called

   _____

4. Knows what FEROCIOUS means

   _____

5. Can name another story about a brave knight

   _____

6. Can name another story about a dragon

   _____

7. Can tell what kind of table King Arthur had

   _____

8. Can name the country where King Arthur's knights were found

   _____

9. Can name a story with a princess

   _____

10. Can name another character who took from the rich and gave to the poor

    _____

SAM, BANGS & MOONSHINE

by Evaline Ness, Holt, 1971

Sam and Bangs live in a fishing community, where their father works with the other men at sea. Sam is warned repeatedly by her father not to tell "moonshine" (as he refers to her tall tales and stories). One day, Sam's father encourages her to go a whole day without indulging in moonshine, and then he's off. While gone, Sam's younger friend Thomas arrives to inquire after her supposed pet of a baby kangaroo. Everyday Thomas asks to see the pet, and everyday Sam tells him that it just left and where Thomas can go to find it. On this particular day Sam sends the boy to a "cave behind Blue Rock." As Thomas leaves Bangs remarks that the tide rises early at Blue Rock that day. Sam doesn't wish to have anything to do with the matter so Bangs goes himself to find Thomas. When the rain begins to fall heavily and neither Thomas nor Bangs returns, Sam gets a rude awakening as to the extent to which moonshine can harm the ones she loves.

FIND SOMEONE WHO . . .

1. Has visited or lives in a fishing community   _____

2. Can name one of the oceans in the world   _____

3. Can tell a story to the group   _____

4. Has gone one whole day without telling an untrue story   _____

5. Has an unusual pet at home   _____

6. Has the nickname Sam   _____

7. Has the first name of Tom or Thomas   _____

8. Has explored a cave   _____

9. Knows in what country you would find a kangaroo   _____

10. Has a cat for a pet   _____

SECTOR 7

by David Wiesner, Clarion, 1999

A young boy in a class visit to the Empire State Building finds that the cloud cover prevents anyone from seeing above or below. The boy makes friends with one happy cloud who takes him into the sky to a place where important-looking officials give the clouds their weather assignments, send the clouds out in huge tubes, and keep track of each cloud on television monitors. Each cloud is given a shape, which it must maintain at all times. The clouds complain to the boy that their assigned shapes are boring. The boy decides to help by giving the clouds new shapes of interesting-looking fish. The angry officials shout at the clouds and tear up the boy's drawings. They send him back to his school group by cloud taxi. The clouds who have enjoyed their newfound freedom continue to take the shape of fish and create a most interesting sky for New Yorkers to look at.

FIND SOMEONE WHO . . .

1. Has gone on a class field trip

2. Knows in what city the Empire State Building is located

3. Has created a picture with squares, triangles, and circles

4. Has found a new way to do a familiar task

5. Can name something that is boring

6. Can name something that is exciting

7. Can draw a picture of a cumulus cloud

8. Can name a place with television monitors

9. Can draw a picture of two different fish

10. Can make up a story about a cloud

SEVEN BLIND MICE

by Ed Young, Philomel, 1992

This is the tale of seven blind mice. Each is a different beautiful color which, of course, they cannot see. One by one, each on a different day of the week, they find and describe a strange object but each describes it differently. To one it is a pillar, to another a snake, to another a cliff. Finally, on the seventh day, the white mouse runs all the way across the thing and remembering what the others found, and decides that it is an elephant. The white mouse shows that the separate parts don't make sense until you put them together to make the whole object.

FIND SOMEONE WHO . . .

1. Can sing the song "Three Blind Mice" _____

2. Has caught a mouse in his or her house _____

3. Likes red as his or her favorite color _____

4. Can draw a picture of a pillar _____

5. Has seen a real elephant _____

6. Can tell the fable of "The Lion and the Mouse" _____

7. Can name the days of the week backward beginning with Sunday _____

8. Likes to work jigsaw puzzles _____

9. Has held a harmless snake in his or her hands _____

10. Can name the three primary colors _____

SHY CHARLES

by Rosemary Wells, Dial, 1988

Charles is happy as a clam and about as talkative as one. His mother is upset that he never says "please" or "thank you." He shies away from football practice and goes to sleep during ballet lessons. One night his parents are out and the baby sitter takes a fall, Charles was playing in his room making a space ship with chairs. He helps the babysitter to the sofa, brings her a blanket and cocoa, and calls the emergency service showing that even the most shy among us can sometimes be big heroes after all.

FIND SOMEONE WHO . . .

1. Is the most quiet person in his or her family

    _____

2. Knows what to say when given a gift

    _____

3. Has Charles as a first name

    _____

4. Knows what to say when asking a favor

    _____

5. Knows what number to dial in an emergency

    _____

6. Has taken ballet lessons

    _____

7. Has watched a real football game

    _____

8. Likes cocoa better than any other hot drink

    _____

9. Has pretended to be a space traveler

    _____

10. Can give a word that is the opposite of SHY

    _____

SIR GAWAIN AND THE GREEN KNIGHT

by Selina Hastings; Illus. by Juan Wijngaard,
Lothrop, Lee & Shepard, 1981

Young Sir Gawain, as yet an untried knight at King Arthur's Round Table, eagerly accepted the challenge of a super-human Green Knight and rode off alone to meet it. His journey was filled with danger and hardship and fear at the trial ahead. But at the end of the journey he was met with a different kind of test and came away wiser for having learned that a true knight must have more than one kind of strength.

FIND SOMEONE WHO . . .

1. Knows the difference between KNIGHT and NIGHT _____

2. Can name a super-human story character _____

3. Has gone on a journey _____

4. Can name something many people fear _____

5. Has taken a test _____

6. Can tell of a hard job he or she has finished _____

7. Can name two ways to be strong _____

8. Has a round table at home _____

9. Can make two new words from the letters in GAWAIN _____

10. Has a first name that begins with the letter G _____

SMOKY NIGHT

by Eve Bunting; Illus. by David Diaz, Harcourt, 1994

Mrs. Kim has a small market shop where Daniel and his mother do not shop. Daniel's mother tells him it is better if we buy from our own people. Mrs. Kim is Asian. Daniel and his mother are African-American. Strangely enough, Daniel's cat and Mrs. Kim's cat don't get along. Then Los Angeles is hit by riots and the apartment building where Daniel and his mother live goes up in flames. For a time Daniel cannot find his cat until he discovers that the neighbors have kept it safe and Daniel learns that when people are in trouble and need help that differences don't matter.

FIND SOMEONE WHO . . .

1. Lives in an apartment building   _____

2. Has Daniel as a first name   _____

3. Has a cat for a pet   _____

4. Knows what number to call in an
   emergency   _____

5. Can tell what to do if a fire starts
   at home   _____

6. Can name two good uses of fire   _____

7. Has lost a pet   _____

8. Has done a favor for a neighbor   _____

9. Has a best friend of a different
   race   _____

10. Knows in what state Los Angeles
    is located   _____

SNOW

by Uri Shulevitz, Farrar, Straus & Giroux, 1998

The radio does not predict snow. The adults say that no snow will fall but the children are hopeful. Watching out the window a little boy sees a snowflake and runs outside with his dog to enjoy the coming winter whiteness. In a short time the flakes are coming down, getting thicker and thicker and seeming to dance and play in the air. A bookshop window adds to the winter scene and three Mother Goose characters step out to play in the snow with the boy and his dog. As the snow continues to fall the drab, gray looking city becomes a winter wonderland.

FIND SOMEONE WHO . . .

1. Likes to play in the snow

       _____

2. Has a dog for a pet

       _____

3. Can name three Mother Goose characters

       _____

4. Can say a Mother Goose rhyme

       _____

5. Has made snow angels

       _____

6. Can say three words that rhyme with SNOW

       _____

7. Has visited a bookshop in the last week

       _____

8. Likes to play outdoors rather than indoors in a cold day

       _____

9. Can sing a song about snow

       _____

10. Can give one reason many adults do not like snow

       _____

THE SNOW QUEEN

by Hans Christian Andersen; Illus. by Susan Jeffers, Dutton, 2006

One day Kay, a small boy, was mysteriously taken away by the Snow Queen, touched as he was by a splinter of glass that turned his heart to glass. Gerda, his sister, went to the Northern Lights in search of Kay. After a long journey she finds Kay and melts his icy heart with a warm teardrop, releasing him from the castle of the Snow Queen.

FIND SOMEONE WHO . . .

1. Can name a story with a queen _____

2. Has gone on a long trip _____

3. Has seen the Northern Lights _____

4. Likes winter better than summer _____

5. Has built a snowman _____

6. Can draw a picture of a castle _____

7. Has a first name that begins with the letter K _____

8. Has a first name that begins with the letter G _____

9. Has one brother _____

10. Has one sister _____

SNOWFLAKE BENTLEY

by Jacqueline Briggs Martin; Illus. by Mary Azarian,
Houghton Mifflin, 1998

Snow in Vermont is as common as dirt. Why would anyone want to photograph it? But from the time he was a small boy, Wilson Bentley thinks of the icy crystals as small miracles and he determines that one day his camera will capture for others their extraordinary beauty. Often misunderstood in his time, Wilson Bentley took pictures that even today reveal two important truths about snowflakes: First, that no two are alike and second, that each one is startlingly beautiful. Here is the story of a simple farmer who not only had a scientist's vision and perseverance, but a clear passion for the wonders of nature.

FIND SOMEONE WHO . . .

1. Can find Vermont on a map _____

2. Has lived on a farm _____

3. Has tasted snowflakes _____

4. Has a set of encyclopedias at home _____

5. Likes to play in the snow _____

6. Can make a paper snowflake _____

7. Knows someone who is home-schooled _____

8. Has built a snow fort _____

9. Can name two words that rhyme with SNOW _____

10. Has taken pictures with a camera _____

THE SNOWY DAY

by Ezra Jack Keats, Viking, 1962

Peter, who lives in an apartment in the city, awakens to find that the snow has fallen overnight. Like any young child, he cannot wait to put on his snowsuit and go outside to explore this winter wonder. Overnight snow plows had cleared the streets, piling huge snowdrifts on the sidewalks. Peter likes the crunching sound his feet make. He find a stick and knocks snow off a nearby tree. He made a snowman and snow angels and slid down a snowdrift. He watched the older children have a snowball fight but knew he was too little to join in. Finally, he packs a snowball as tightly as he can and puts it in his pocket to play with the next day. Of course, when he awakens the next morning his pocket is empty but, to his joy, the snow is falling again.

FIND SOMEONE WHO . . .

1. Lives in or has visited a big city _____

2. Can tell what a snow plow does _____

3. Can say two words that rhyme with SNOW _____

4. Can name another story character named Peter _____

5. Has made a snow angel _____

6. Can name three things to wear in the snow _____

7. Likes hot oatmeal for breakfast _____

8. Has built a snowman _____

9. Lives in an apartment _____

10. Can name three things to do in the snow _____

SO YOU WANT TO BE PRESIDENT?

by Judith St. George; Illus. by David Small, Philomel, 2000

Being the president of the United States is a big job and getting bigger. Presidents have come in just about every variety. From the embarrassment of skinny-dipping John Quincy Adams, to the escapades of Theodore Roosevelt's children, to the heroic recovery of John Kennedy's crew, the author shares the backroom facts, the spitfire comments, and the comical anecdotes that have been part and parcel of the White House.

FIND SOMEONE WHO . . .

1. Can name the president of the United States

2. Has spent a night in a log cabin

3. Is taking piano lessons

4. Likes to read books

5. Can name three former U.S. presidents

6. Knows where the U.S. president lives

7. Knows someone in the military

8. Has an unusual pet

9. Has gone swimming in a river

10. Can name two jobs of a president

SOMETHING SPECIAL FOR ME

by Vera B. Williams, Greenwillow, 1983

Rosa has a birthday coming up in three days. The money Mama has put in the jar from her tips at the Blue Tile Diner is to buy something special for Rosa. Rosa and her mother go shopping and Rosa sees new skates, a polka dot dress with new shoes, and a blue sleeping bag. All three would be very nice to have but not really special. The tired shoppers stop at the Blue Tile Diner for pie and ice cream before going home. Rosa worries that she can't decide on what is truly special before her birthday comes. She looks up at the night sky and wishes on a star that she would know what to ask for. On the way home Rosa hears music and sees a man under a lamppost playing an accordion. Rosa listens to the music and knows what her most special wish will be. A trip to the music store on her birthday results in an accordion just her size. Rosa can't wait to begin lessons and make beautiful music come.

FIND SOMEONE WHO . . .

1. Has a birthday this month _____

2. Knows a waiter or waitress _____

3. Has a jar or bank of coins _____

4. Is learning to play an instrument _____

5. Has gone downtown shopping _____

6. Knows how to ice skate _____

7. Is wearing a piece of clothing
   with polka dots _____

8. Has a blue sleeping bag _____

9. Knows what a jukebox is _____

10. Knows someone who plays an ac-
    cordion _____

SONG AND DANCE MAN

by Karen Ackerman; Illus. by Stephen Gammell, Knopf, 1992

Once a song and dance man, Grandpa reclaims his youth and profession before the delighted eyes of his three grandchildren one afternoon. He simply cannot resist the urge to dress up in clothes left over from his vaudeville days—complete with top hat and gold-headed cane—and to perform tricks, play the banjo, and tell jokes. He taps, twirls, and laughs himself to tears on a thrown-together stage in his attic.

FIND SOMEONE WHO . . .

1. Has more than one grandfather _____

2. Can sing a song for the group _____

3. Can play a musical instrument _____

4. Can perform a dance for the group _____

5. Has taken tap dancing lessons _____

6. Has an attic in his or her house _____

7. Has laughed until he or she cried _____

8. Can perform a trick for the group _____

9. Can tell a funny story _____

10. Has watched real singers and dancers on a stage _____

SONG OF THE SWALLOWS

by Leo Politi, Scribners, 1987

Every summer the swallows leave San Juan Capistrano and fly far away to a peaceful green island, but they always come back in the spring on St. Joseph's Day. Juan loves las golondrinas, and so does his friend, Julian the gardener at the mission. This year, Juan plants a garden in his own yard. There is nothing he wants more than for the swallows to nest there. And on St. Joseph's Day, his dream comes true.

FIND SOMEONE WHO . . .

1. Is the smallest child in his or her family

   _____

2. Has helped to plant a garden

   _____

3. Knows in what direction birds fly in winter

   _____

4. Knows what a legend is

   _____

5. Can find California on a map

   _____

6. Can say "Hello" in Spanish

   _____

7. Can recall a good dream

   _____

8. Can name two colors in a sunset

   _____

9. Has visited or lived in California

   _____

10. Can make three new words from the letters in SWALLOW

    _____

THE STAR CHILD

by Oscar Wilde; Illus. by Fiona French, Atheneum, 1979

Two woodcutters watched a star fall out of the sky and land in the pine forest where they were. When they reached the place where the star had fallen they found a baby wrapped in golden tissue. One took the baby home, where he was brought up with the village children and every year grew more beautiful, vain, and selfish. As the child of a star he was filled with pride. One day he accidentally met his real mother and spurned her because she was old and ugly and clothed in rags. For this cruel act he was changed into a creature as ugly as a toad and must wander the world until he learns humility and compassion.

FIND SOMEONE WHO . . .

1. Has a pine tree in his or her yard

    _____

2. Has wished on a star

    _____

3. Can say a poem about a star

    _____

4. Lives or has lived in a small town or village

    _____

5. Has seen a falling star

    _____

6. Has a baby brother or sister

    _____

7. Has an older person for a friend

    _____

8. Can say two words that rhyme with STAR

    _____

9. Can name something the color of gold

    _____

10. Can name two beautiful things in nature

    _____

STARRY MESSENGER

by Peter Sis, Farrar, Straus & Giroux, 1996

In this picture-book biography of Galileo Galilei we are introduced to a bright and curious child who, as his education progressed, was especially talented in the fields of mathematics and physics. He developed a telescope that could magnify an image 20 times and used it to study the stars. He recorded his observations in a book titled *The Starry Messenger*. The book received much attention and unfortunately caught the attention of church officials. In proposing that the Earth was at the center of the universe, Galileo spoke in direct conflict with the teachings of the church. He was tried and sentenced to remain a prisoner in his own home for the rest of his life. Three hundred years later he was pardoned when science upheld his theories.

FIND SOMEONE WHO . . .

1. Has been in trouble for being curious

   _____

2. Likes math better than any other subject

   _____

3. Can name the planet we call home

   _____

4. Has seen a shooting star

   _____

5. Knows what makes night and day

   _____

6. Can name two planets other than Earth

   _____

7. Knows what a telescope is used for

   _____

8. Can name three words that rhyme with STAR

   _____

9. Can sing a song about a star

   _____

10. Likes to watch the stars at night

   _____

STELLALUNA

by Janell Cannon, Harcourt, 1993

Mother bat is flying one night when she meets an owl. In her attempts to escape the bird she drops her baby, Stellaluna. The young bat lands in a bird's nest where she is adopted by a mother bird. Stellaluna is fed insects (which she hates) and taught to sit on a branch right side up. "Following the house rules," says Mother Bird, "is very important." Stellaluna finally meets a family of bats and is recognized by her own mother. The bat family teaches her bat ways that include flying at night and eating sweet fruit as well as hanging upside-down to sleep. When Stellaluna and the birds meet again they discover that they are both very alike and very different and that this does not keep them from becoming friends.

FIND SOMEONE WHO . . .

1. Has heard an owl hoot   _____

2. Has walked in the woods at night   _____

3. Got lost from his or her parent   _____

4. Has seen a real bat   _____

5. Can name one thing both a bat and a bird can do   _____

6. Knows how a bat sleeps   _____

7. Knows what LUNA means   _____

8. Can say an important rule to follow   _____

9. Can name five words that rhyme with BAT   _____

10. Likes oranges better than any other fruit   _____

THE STINKY CHEESE MAN AND
OTHER FAIRLY STUPID TALES

by Jon Scieszka; Illus. by Lane Smith, Viking, 1992

Here are ten traditional tales told as they have never been told before. Each has a unique twist from the original. Instead of a falling sky, Chicken Licken sees a falling table of contents. The ugly duckling is really a very ugly duck. Nobody wanted to chase the Stinky Cheese Man and instead of a foot race, the hare challenges the tortoise to a hair-growing contest. Cinderella and Rumpelstiltskin end up in the same story and to add to the chaos, the print in the book can be large, small, upside-down, and sideways. It is a book full of surprises and one to look at again and again as new discoveries are made. The silly stories may inspire older readers to try creating twisted tales of their own.

FIND SOMEONE WHO . . .

1. Likes gingerbread cookies _____

2. Can name two fairy tale characters _____

3. Knows who said, "The sky is falling!" _____

4. Has a frog for a pet _____

5. Can name a story with a princess _____

6. Knows what was under the mattress the real princess slept on _____

7. Has been lost at least once _____

8. Has seen a real fox _____

9. Knows what kind of bird the Ugly Duckling turned out to be _____

10. Can make three new words using the letters in CINDERELLA _____

A STORY, A STORY

by Gail E. Haley, Atheneum, 1970

The African storyteller begins: "We do not really mean, we do not really mean that what we are about to say is true. A Story, a story; let it come, let it go." And it tells that long, long ago there were no stories on Earth for children to hear. All stories belonged to Nyame, the Sky God. Ananse, the Spider man, wanted to buy some of these stories, so he spun a web up to the sky and went up to bargain with the Sky God. The price the Sky God asked was Osebo, the leopard of-the-terrible-teeth; Mmboro, the hornet who-stings-like-fire; and Mmoatia, the fairy whom-men-never-see. How Ananse manages to pay the price makes a fascinating story.

FIND SOMEONE WHO . . .

1. Can name someone who is a good storyteller

    _____

2. Can tell a story to the group

    _____

3. Can find Africa on a map

    _____

4. Has seen a real leopard at the zoo

    _____

5. Has run away from a hornet

    _____

6. Can draw a picture of a spider

    _____

7. Has played a trick on someone

    _____

8. Can name an animal with terrible teeth

    _____

9. Can name two other African animals

    _____

10. Knows what it means to bargain

    _____

THE STRANGER

by Chris Van Allsburg, Houghton Mifflin, 1986

It was the end of summer when Farmer Bailey hit the man with his truck. Suddenly the man got to his feet and tried to flee, but when he fell again, Farmer Bailey helped him into his truck and took him home to his family. Because the stranger was unable to speak, the doctor was called. He could find no major injuries and recommended rest for a few days. Everyday things in the home puzzled the stranger. When he blew on his soup to cool it the family felt a cold draft in the room. The stranger worked in the fields with Farmer Bailey until the end of summer. Walking to the top of a hill he saw a strange sight. The trees in the distance had changed color to oranges and browns but the trees surrounding the Bailey farm were still green. He picked up a leaf and blew on it. The next day he told the family goodbye. The air had turned cold, and the leaves on the trees were no longer green. Since the stranger's visit, the trees around the Bailey farm remain green longer than those in the distance and etched in frost on the farmhouse window are words that say, "See you next fall."

FIND SOMEONE WHO . . .

1. Can give two possible reasons a person does not speak _____

2. Can name three signs of changing seasons _____

3. Knows what a pitchfork is used for _____

4. Has ridden in a truck _____

5. Has visited or lived on a farm _____

6. Can name one daily chore on a farm _____

7. Can explain what a hermit is _____

8. Can name a state with only one season _____

9. Has helped someone who was hurt _____

10. Can say three words that rhyme with FALL _____

THE STRAY DOG: FROM A TRUE STORY BY REIKO SASSA

by Marc Simont, HarperCollins, 2001

A friendly dog approaches a family out for a picnic in the country. The children name the dog Willy and want to take him home but the parents say no. The next weekend the family picnics in the same place. The brother and sister see a dog catcher who plans to capture the dog because it has no collar or leash and must not belong to anyone. The boy takes off his belt and the girl takes off her hair ribbon explaining to the dog catcher that these are Willy's collar and leash and that the dog belongs to them. The parents relent and Willy is taken home, given a bath, and introduced to all the other neighborhood dogs.

FIND SOMEONE WHO . . .

1. Has gone on a picnic with his or her family

   _____

2. Has taken a stray animal home

   _____

3. Has a dog for a pet

   _____

4. Has given a dog a bath

   _____

5. Has one brother

   _____

6. Has one sister

   _____

7. Is wearing a hair ribbon

   _____

8. Is wearing a belt

   _____

9. Has the first name of William

   _____

10. Can name three words that rhyme with STRAY

    _____

STREGA NONA

by Tomie dePaola, Simon & Schuster, 1975

In the town of Calabria, there lived an old lady everyone called Strega Nona, which meant Grandma Witch. The town would go to see her if they had troubles. Because Strega Nona was getting old she needed help, she put up a help-wanted sign in the town square. Big Anthony who didn't pay attention went to see her and started working for Strega Nona. But there was one condition: he must never touch her cooking pot. However, in her absence he says the magic words that cause the pot to cook. Pasta is everywhere! Unfortunately, Big Anthony does not know the words to turn the pot off. Imagine what happens when Strega Nona returns!

FIND SOMEONE WHO . . .

1. Can find Italy on a map 　　＿＿＿＿＿＿＿＿＿＿＿＿＿＿＿

2. Can name a story with a witch 　＿＿＿＿＿＿＿＿＿＿＿＿＿＿＿

3. Has lived in a small town 　　＿＿＿＿＿＿＿＿＿＿＿＿＿＿＿

4. Has Anthony or Tony as a first name 　＿＿＿＿＿＿＿＿＿＿＿＿＿＿＿

5. Likes to eat pasta 　　　＿＿＿＿＿＿＿＿＿＿＿＿＿＿＿

6. Can say some magic words 　　＿＿＿＿＿＿＿＿＿＿＿＿＿＿＿

7. Has helped an older person do a job 　＿＿＿＿＿＿＿＿＿＿＿＿＿＿＿

8. Has more than one grandma 　　＿＿＿＿＿＿＿＿＿＿＿＿＿＿＿

9. Is the tallest person in the class or group 　＿＿＿＿＿＿＿＿＿＿＿＿＿＿＿

10. Can make a new word from the letters in POT 　＿＿＿＿＿＿＿＿＿＿＿＿＿＿＿

STREGA NONA'S MAGIC LESSONS

by Tomie dePaola, Harcourt, 1982

Strega Nona had two pupils for her magic lessons. One was Bambolona, the town baker's daughter, and the other was Antonia, who was really Strega Nona's helper, Big Anthony, dressed up like a girl. Bambolona learned quickly and well. Big Anthony was not a very good student. When Strega Nona gives Bambolona a book containing more magic spells, Big Anthony tries to surprise Strega Nona by learning magic on his own. All he manages to do is to turn her into a frog, which did not please her at all. Big Anthony again learns an important lesson . . . not to do magic until you have learned very well.

FIND SOMEONE WHO . . .

1. Can do a magic trick _____

2. Can tell something new he or she has learned _____

3. Can name a story that has a good witch _____

4. Has an older person as a friend _____

5. Has more than one book at home _____

6. Has caught a frog _____

7. Can tell of a time when he or she has been surprised _____

8. Has tried to learn do do something without help _____

9. Can name a food to buy at a bakery _____

10. Knows a girl named Antonia _____

SUSANNA OF THE ALAMO

by John Jakes; Illus. by Paul Bacon, Harcourt, Brace, Jovanovich, 1986

The North Americans who lived in Texas declared independence from Mexico on March 2, 1836. One week before, General Santa Anna, with 4000 men, marched into San Antonio. All the citizens of that town had taken refuge in the Alamo, which was defended by 182 men including 12 Tennessee volunteers brought by 50-year-old Davy Crockett. On March 6, 1836 Santa Anna led 4000 of his tough infantry men a siege against the Texans' small force at the Alamo. The 182 brave defenders fought hand-to-hand with sticks, bayonets, rifle butts, and fists, but all were killed. Only the women and children huddled together in the sacristy were saved. One of these women, Susanna Dickinson, told the Alamo story to the world.

FIND SOMEONE WHO . . .

1. Has a first name beginning with S

   _____

2. Has a birthday in March

   _____

3. Can find Texas on a map

   _____

4. Has Davy or David as a first name

   _____

5. Knows what a sacristy is

   _____

6. Has taken shelter in a storm

   _____

7. Can name 4000 of something that would fit in a shoebox

   _____

8. Knows what it means to take refuge

   _____

9. Can name something you would buy a dozen of

   _____

10. Can name two countries in North America

   _____

SWAMP ANGEL

by Anne Isaacs; Illus. by Paul O. Zelinsky, Dutton, 1994

When Angelica Longrider was born, she was scarcely taller than her mother and couldn't climb a tree without help. She was a full two years old before she built her first log cabin. But by the time she is fully grown, Swamp Angel, as she is known, can lasso a tornado and drink an entire lake dry. She single-handedly saves the settlers from the fearsome bear known as Thundering Tarnation, wrestling him from the top of the Great Smoky Mountains to the bottom of a deep lake. It was a fight that lasted five days. When both Swamp Angel and the bear were too tired to fight, they went to sleep and Swamp Angel's snores were so loud that she snored down a huge tree that landed on the bear and killed it. Swamp Angel paid tribute to her foe and then had enough bear meat to feed everyone in Tennessee.

FIND SOMEONE WHO . . .

1. Can climb a tree without help

    _____

2. Has been inside a real log cabin

    _____

3. Can tell you where to go when there is a tornado warning

    _____

4. Can say the name of a real lake

    _____

5. Can name a story about a bear

    _____

6. Has climbed up a mountain

    _____

7. Knows what a swamp is

    _____

8. Can find Tennessee on a map

    _____

9. Can name another tall tale hero

    _____

10. Has a first name that begins with the letter A

    _____

SWEET CLARA AND THE FREEDOM QUILT

by Deborah Hopkinson; Illus. by James Ransome, Knopf, 1993

When young Clara is taken from her mother and sent to work in the fields at the Home Plantation she is broken-hearted. A kindly woman she calls Aunt Rachel looks after the child and teaches her to sew, insisting on the finest small stitches. Clara discovers why Aunt Rachel is so particular when she is taken to the Big House to show her work to the Master's wife. She becomes a seamstress in the Big House. Clara is a good listener. When she hears other slaves talking about reaching the Underground Railroad to seek freedom in Canada, she begins to make a map, a quilt she patiently sews year after year. When the quilt is finally finished it shows the rivers, creeks, fields, other plantations, and finally, the route to take to freedom. During a thunderstorm Clara and her friend Jack escape, following the route she now carries in her head. She leaves the quilt with Aunt Rachel for others to follow.

FIND SOMEONE WHO . . .

1. Has had to keep a secret _____

2. Has traveled a long distance at night _____

3. Has moved to a new house _____

4. Has pulled weeds in a garden _____

5. Knows what a seamstress is _____

6. Can name an animal that lives in a swamp _____

7. Has an aunt whose first name begins with the letter R _____

8. Can find Canada on a map _____

9. Is a good listener _____

10. Has walked across a field to a river _____

SYLVESTER AND THE MAGIC PEBBLE

by William Steig, Simon & Schuster, 1969

Sylvester, the donkey, loves to collect beautiful pebbles. One day he comes upon a magic pebble that will grant him anything he wishes. On his way home to share his discovery, a lion frightens him. Without thinking, Sylvester wishes to become a rock. When he does not return home his worried parents go to the police for help but no one can find Sylvester. In the spring Sylvester's father takes his mother on a picnic. She picks up a pebble and places it on a large stone, which happens to be Sylvester who becomes a donkey again.

FIND SOMEONE WHO . . .

1. Has gone on a picnic with his or her family

   _____

2. Can tell a time when he or she has been lost

   _____

3. Likes to collect rocks

   _____

4. Likes fall best of all the seasons

   _____

5. Can name something fun to do on a rainy day

   _____

6. Has seen a real donkey

   _____

7. Has wished upon a star

   _____

8. Has seen a lion at the zoo

   _____

9. Can give a reason to call the police

   _____

10. Has tried to move a very large stone

    _____

THE TALKING EGGS

by Robert San Souci; Illus. by Jerry Pinkney, Dial, 1989

This southern folktale is about two sisters, Rose, who is lazy and mean but her mother's favorite, and Blanche, who is sweet and kind but treated harshly and made to do all the work. Blanche's unhappy life is changed when she befriends an old woman with magical powers. She is taken to an unusual world of two-headed cows, rainbow-colored chickens, and wonderful talking eggs. Blanche's goodness is rewarded as she discovers that beauty can be found in the simplest of things.

FIND SOMEONE WHO . . .

1. Can name a girl's name that is a flower

   _____

2. Can name two southern states in the United States

   _____

3. Knows another story about a girl who must do all the work at home

   _____

4. Can name a tale where someone has magical powers

   _____

5. Has spent time on a farm

   _____

6. Likes scrambled eggs best for breakfast

   _____

7. Can name three words that rhyme with HEN

   _____

8. Can name three beautiful things found in nature

   _____

9. Can tell how he or she has helped an older person

   _____

10. Can say a word that is the opposite of lazy

    _____

TAR BEACH

by Faith Ringgold, Crown Publishers, 1991

Eight-year-old Cassie lives in New York City in Harlem where she lets her imagination soar as the family spends summer evenings on the rooftop of their apartment building. In her mind she flies through the sky over the George Washington Bridge (which she claims as her own), and dreams of being rich some day. She tells of her dad who works on steel girders in tall buildings and wants her dad to be a union member. She knows this can't be because his father was not. In Cassie's dream world, her mother can sleep late and there will be ice cream for dessert every night. These are her dreams as she makes her nightly flight over Tar Beach.

FIND SOMEONE WHO . . .

1. Has lived in or visited New York City

2. Has walked on top of an apartment building

3. Can name something named after our first president

4. Knows what a union is

5. Likes strawberry ice cream best

6. Has spent part of a vacation on a beach

7. Can name two things found only in a big city

8. Can make up a four-word sentence about Cassie with each word beginning with the letter C

9. Has flown in a real airplane

10. Has an eight-year-old sister

TIKKI TIKKI TEMBO

by Arlene Mosel; Illus. by Blair Lent, Holt, 1968

Long ago the Chinese gave their first-born sons very long names. Tikki tikki tembo-no sa rembo-chari bari ruchi-pip peri pembo is the full name of a boy who falls in a well. When his younger brother attempts to get help, he has a hard time saying the name and help is delayed with surprising results.

FIND SOMEONE WHO . . .

1. Has the longest last name in the group or class

   _____

2. Can find China on a map

   _____

3. Has a younger brother

   _____

4. Can draw a picture of a well

   _____

5. Has climbed a ladder

   _____

6. Has eaten a rice cake

   _____

7. Has forgotten to give someone a message

   _____

8. Has won a race by running fast

   _____

9. Has had a good dream come true

   _____

10. Knows someone who comes from China

    _____

TOPS AND BOTTOMS

by Janet Stevens, Harcourt, 1995

Instead of planting crops for the coming winter, bear can't be bothered and sleeps the planting time away. Hare talks to bear and tells him that hare and his family will plant bear's crops and asks bear if he wants the tops or the bottoms of the crops because they are to share the crops equally. Bear asks for the tops and hare plants root bottoms (like potatoes) leaving bear with nothing to eat. The next season bear asks for the bottoms and goes to sleep in his favorite chair. Clever hare plants corn, again leaving lazy bear with nothing to eat.

FIND SOMEONE WHO . . .

1. Can name two vegetables that grow under the ground

2. Can name two vegetables that grow above the ground

3. Knows another story about a bear

4. Can sing a song about a bear

5. Has gone to sleep when there was a job to be done

6. Can give an animal name that rhymes with BEAR

7. Knows what real bears do in the winter

8. Can name two dishes made with corn

9. Likes mashed potatoes better than fries

10. Can say a word that is the opposite of CLEVER

THE TRUE STORY OF THE THREE LITTLE PIGS

by Jon Scieszka; Illus. by Lane Smith, Viking, 1989

Here is the traditional Three Little Pigs tale retold by A. Wolf who wants readers to know what really happened. It seems that he wanted to make a birthday cake for his granny and needed to borrow some sugar from his closest neighbors, the pigs. However, A. Wolf had a bad cold and just before he could make his request for sugar, he sneezed so hard that he blew down the houses of the first two pigs. Not wanting to waste a perfectly good ham dinner, the wolf ate the pigs. However, when he tried to borrow sugar from the third pig with a house of bricks, the third pig called the police and the wolf ended up in jail. Not his fault at all, to hear him tell it.

FIND SOMEONE WHO . . .

1. Has celebrated a grandparent's birthday

2. Can name something he or she has borrowed

3. Can name another story with a wolf

4. Has had to stay in bed with a bad cold

5. Has sneezed three times in a row

6. Likes ham better than any other meat

7. Can give one reason to call the police

8. Can say a word that rhymes with JAIL

9. Can say a Mother Goose rhyme about a pig

10. Has a last name that begins with the letter P or W

THE UGLY DUCKLING

by Hans Christian Andersen; Illus. by Jerry Pinkney,
William Morrow, 1999

When mother duck's egg hatches it is different from the rest. The huge duckling must be a turkey chick! The other fowl on the farm chase, peck, and kick the poor duckling. He runs away from the pond and finds the warm cottage of an old woman with a cat and a hen. However he misses the water and heads out again into the cold autumn world. He sees a flock of swans flying overhead and wishes he could be like those beautiful creatures. Finally after a hard winter he sees the swans again and to his surprise, they welcome him! And when he looks in the water, he sees the beautiful swan he has become.

FIND SOMEONE WHO . . .

1. Has watched eggs hatch

   _____

2. Knows another story by Hans Christian Andersen

   _____

3. Has lived on or visited a farm

   _____

4. Has taken a stray animal home

   _____

5. Has watched ducks swimming on a pond

   _____

6. Can name two other pond animals

   _____

7. Has had a duck or chicken as a pet

   _____

8. Can name two differences between swans and ducks

   _____

9. Has found a egg that has fallen from its nest

   _____

10. Likes winter better than any other season

   _____

UNCLE JED'S BARBERSHOP

by Margaree King Mitchell; Illus. by James Ransome, Simon & Schuster, 1993

Sarah Jean's Uncle Jed was the only black barber in the county. He had a kind heart and a warm smile. And he had a dream. Living in the segregated South of the 1920s, where most people were sharecroppers, Uncle Jed had to travel all over the county to cut his customers' hair. He lived for the day when he could open his very own barbershop. But it was a long time, and many setbacks, from the five-year-old Sarah Jean's operation to the bank failures of the Great Depression, before the joyful day when Uncle Jed opened his shiny new shop, and twirled a now grown-up Sarah Jean around in the barber chair.

FIND SOMEONE WHO . . .

1. Has the first name of Sarah _____

2. Can name a favorite relative _____

3. Has more than one uncle _____

4. Can name the colors on a barber pole _____

5. Has had an operation _____

6. Can name three ways to travel other than a car _____

7. Can name something worth more than $300.00 _____

8. Has a middle name of Jean _____

9. Does not like to get a haircut _____

10. Has never had a haircut _____

THE VELVETEEN RABBIT

by Margery Williams, Doubleday & Company, 1991

The boy received the Velveteen Rabbit as a Christmas gift but it was soon forgotten when the shiny mechanical toys were unwrapped. The Rabbit ended up in the nursery cupboard with the other toys who wanted little to do with him. The Rabbit's one friend was the Skin Horse who was so old that his brown coat was bald in places. The Skin Horse had seen many mechanical toys come and go and assured the Velveteen Rabbit that being real "isn't how you are made. It's a thing that happens to you." The Rabbit is put in the boy's bed one night. After that the boy cannot sleep without him and although his fur was getting shabbier he discovers that he is REAL to the boy who will not go anywhere without him. The boy becomes very ill and all the toys that are full of germs, including the Velveteen Rabbit, must be burned. Tears fall from the rabbit and as they touch the ground a beautiful flower blooms. From the flower emerges a lovely fairy. Her kiss changes the rabbit and makes him real. She takes him to a place where real rabbits live and with a leap of joy he joins them.

FIND SOMEONE WHO . . .

1. Has a stuffed animal   _____

2. Has a mechanical toy   _____

3. Knows what INSIGNIFICANT means   _____

4. Can name two different flowers   _____

5. Can name a fairy in another story   _____

6. Has visited or lived near an ocean   _____

7. Has had to stay in bed a week or more due to an illness   _____

8. Has gone walking in the woods   _____

9. Has seen real rabbits playing in the wild   _____

10. Can name his or her favorite toy   _____

THE VERY HUNGRY CATERPILLAR

by Eric Carle, Philomel, 1969

Imagine how exciting it would be to travel on an adventuresome journey into the life of a caterpillar. It certainly would be interesting to experience all the changes a caterpillar goes through from the time it is hatched from an egg, to when it spins a chrysalis, until it emerges as a beautiful butterfly. On a beautiful, sunny Sunday morning a little egg does hatch and out comes a green, fuzzy caterpillar. This caterpillar was very hungry so he ate everything he could find, including cake and pickles. In fact, the caterpillar ate so much that he got a stomachache but before he could spin his cocoon he had to eat something else. Can you guess what it was?

FIND SOMEONE WHO . . .

1. Has found a caterpillar on a leaf   _____

2. Has had a pickle for breakfast   _____

3. Likes strawberries better than any other fruit   _____

4. Has had a stomachache from eating too much   _____

5. Knows what a chrysalis is   _____

6. Can name the days of the week   _____

7. Knows another creature that changes its form   _____

8. Can name two things that hatch from eggs   _____

9. Can find two other words in CATERPILLAR   _____

10. Can find a picture of a butterfly in the encyclopedia   _____

THE VILLAGE OF ROUND AND SQUARE HOUSES
by Ann Grifalconi, Little Brown, 1986

Imagine if your town were sitting at the foot of a volcano. This is exactly where the village of Tos in West Central Africa sits. The people of the village lead simple lives. During the day they work in the fields. The women prepare the evening meal which is shared by all. After the meal Grandma Tika smokes her pipe and tells a story to eager listeners. It seems that long ago the volcano in the Naka Mountain erupted and rained down upon the village with orange fire and gray ash. None of the villagers were hurt but all were covered with the gray ash. All of the houses in the village were destroyed except for two, one round house and one square house. The village chief, unable to tell who his ash-covered subjects were, assigned the "tall gray things" (men) to live in the square house, and the "round gray things" (women) to live in the round house. To this day, that is the way the villagers live.

FIND SOMEONE WHO . . .

1. Lives or has lived in a very small town

   _____

2. Can find Africa on a map

   _____

3. Can name four things that are round

   _____

4. Can name four things that are square

   _____

5. Has a grandmother who tells stories

   _____

6. Would rather listen to a storyteller than watch TV

   _____

7. Has helped his or her mother prepare supper

   _____

8. Can name a food that grows in a field

   _____

9. Has hiked up a mountain

   _____

10. Knows someone who smokes a pipe

    _____

THE WAGON

by Tony Johnston; Illus. by James E. Ransome, **Boyds Mill Press, 1996**

On a Carolina spring morning a child is born into slavery. He grows, and is soon working find the cotton fields from dawn to dark. The boy would rather be free to play but must carry wood and help his father, a carpenter, build a wagon. The boy is often in trouble because of his resentment and has trouble watching his tongue. And as he grows, he dreams that he and President Lincoln are chopping wood together and that the wagon he has helped build for Master is a glorious chariot to freedom.

FIND SOMEONE WHO . . .

1. Is wearing something made of cotton   _____

2. Has helped his or her father build something   _____

3. Can name a job that takes a whole day to complete   _____

4. Has had a dream that came true   _____

5. Has ridden in a wagon   _____

6. Has said words he or she should not have said   _____

7. Knows what a carpenter does   _____

8. Knows what FREEDOM means   _____

9. Knows the birthday of Abraham Lincoln   _____

10. Knows about how many hours it is from dawn until dark   _____

THE WALL

by Eve Bunting; Illus. by Ronald Himler, Houghton Mifflin, 1990

A young boy and his father visit the Vietnam Memorial, a shiny black wall that lists the names of those killed and missing in the Vietnam War. They have come to find the name of the boy's grandfather and when they do find it, they make a rubbing of it. While they are there, many other visitors come to the wall, some to search, some to stand in silent tribute, and some to leave small mementos. The boy sees a veteran in a wheelchair, an elderly couple, and a group of school children with their teacher. The father carefully puts away the rubbing of grandfather's name and leaves a picture of the boy at the foot of the wall. The boy notes that the wall is a sad place to visit but his father tells him it is also a place of honor and that he is proud to find grandpa's name there.

FIND SOMEONE WHO . . .

1. Can name a famous memorial _____

2. Can find Vietnam on a map _____

3. Has taken a class trip _____

4. Has made a rubbing from a tomb-
   stone _____

5. Knows what a memorial is _____

6. Can tell you where the Vietnam
   Memorial is located _____

7. Can name the capital of the
   United States _____

8. Has taken a trip to another state _____

9. Has taken a trip with his or her
   father _____

10. Flies the American flag some-
    where at home _____

WHEN I WAS YOUNG IN THE MOUNTAINS

by Cynthia Rylant; Illus. by Diane Goode, Dutton, 1985

A little girl tells of her life with her grandparents in the Appalachian mountains. Grandfather is a coal miner and often comes home covered with black coal dust. The swimming hole was sometimes dark and muddy and swimmers often had snakes for companions but they swam anyway. With no running water, water had to be taken from the well and heated in large tubs for baths. But regardless of the primitive life, the mountains hold a special allure for the child and she would not live anywhere else if given a choice.

FIND SOMEONE WHO . . .

1. Has climbed a mountain _____

2. Has seen a real snake _____

3. Has had a bath in a tin tub _____

4. Likes cocoa _____

5. Knows what okra is _____

6. Can name a state that has a coal
   mine _____

7. Can find Virginia on a map _____

8. Has gone swimming in a creek _____

9. Has more than one grandparent _____

10. Has had a snake for a pet _____

WHERE THE WILD THINGS ARE

by Maurice Sendak, HarperCollins, 1963

Max has misbehaved. He is sent to his room to think things over and his imaginative mind dreams up a river, a boat, and a forest. He sails away to an imaginary kingdom where there are no parents to send you to your room. Max's room becomes a kingdom with tall trees and wild things. Max, as king of the wild things, orders the rumpus to begin and romps through the forest with the scary looking creatures. After the romp he returns to his room where supper might be waiting after all.

FIND SOMEONE WHO . . .

1. Has a first name that begins with the letter M _____

2. Can name two real wild animals _____

3. Has had to take a time-out _____

4. Has a younger brother _____

5. Can draw a picture of a wild thing _____

6. Can name a real ocean _____

7. Has run through a forest _____

8. Has climbed a tall tree _____

9. Has ridden on the back of an animal _____

10. Can name a king in a Mother Goose rhyme _____

WHITE SNOW, BRIGHT SNOW

by Alvin Tresselt; Illus. by Roger Duvoisin, Lothrop, Lee & Shepard, 1947

The postman, the farmer, the policeman, the children, and even the rabbits knew it was going to snow. And sure enough from the low, grey sky the snowflakes came: first one, then two, then a whole sky full. By evening the whole town was covered with the snowflakes that the children had tried to catch on their tongues. By morning automobiles looked like big fat raisins buried in snowdrifts. The postman put on his high boots, the farmer milked his cows, the policeman stayed in bed with a chill, and the children made a snowman. As the days passed the snow disappeared and signs of spring emerged from small flowers, to sunshine, to the first call of a robin.

FIND SOMEONE WHO . . .

1. Likes to play in the snow

    _____

2. Has built a snowman

    _____

3. Has been in a snowball fight

    _____

4. Knows the name of the person who brings his or her mail

    _____

5. Has lived on or visited a farm

    _____

6. Knows where milk comes from

    _____

7. Has had to take cough medicine

    _____

8. Has had to stay in bed for a day

    _____

9. Has caught a snowflake on the tongue

    _____

10. Likes winter better than any other season

    _____

WHY MOSQUITOES BUZZ IN PEOPLE'S EARS

by Verna Aardema; Illus. by Leo and Diane Dillon, Dial, 1975

One morning a mosquito tells an iguana a foolish tale that he doesn't want to hear. The iguana puts sticks in his ears and storms off. He passes a python and doesn't say good morning. The python thinks the iguana is mad at him so he slithers down into a rabbit's den. This begins confusion throughout the jungle and ends when Mother Owl refuses to wake the sun. Mosquito, however, finds he has to pay for his foolishness.

FIND SOMEONE WHO . . .

1. Can tell a funny story _____

2. Can name something most people fear _____

3. Can name the number of letters in AFRICA _____

4. Can tell about a job done well _____

5. Has chased a crow away _____

6. Knows what the lion is king of _____

7. Knows someone who wears a hearing aid _____

8. Knows someone who has been hurt in an accident _____

9. Can make a new word with the letters in OWL _____

10. Has played the telephone game _____

WILLIAM'S DOLL

by Charlotte Zolotow; Illus. by William Pene du Bois,
Harper & Row, 1972, Reprinted in HarperCollins
Treasury of Picture Book Classics, 2003

William's brother called him a creep. The boy next door called him a sissy. Why? Because William wanted a doll like the one that belonged to Nancy next door. William was good at shooting a basketball the way his father taught him. He played a lot with his train. But he still wanted a doll and told his grandmother so. She bought William a doll with along white dress and a bonnet. She bought it so that William could learn to care for and love a baby as all good fathers should.

FIND SOMEONE WHO . . .

1. Has a first name of William or Bill

   _____

2. Can shoot a basketball into a basket

   _____

3. Plays with a train set at home

   _____

4. Has a friend named Nancy

   _____

5. Thinks only girls should play with dolls

   _____

6. Has more than one grandmother

   _____

7. Thinks shooting baskets is only for boys

   _____

8. Likes many sports

   _____

9. Can say a word that is the opposite of SISSY

   _____

10. Can name something a good father does

    _____

ZATHURA

by Chris Van Allsburg, Houghton Mifflin, 2002

Imagine a game that could take you down a black hole, whiz you through outer space, and let you tangle with a defective robot! When Walter had to look after his little brother while their parents went out to dinner, Walter was not happy. He wanted to watch television but Danny wanted to play catch. A chase through the park ends up with Walter finding a board game hidden under another board game. The name of the game was Zathura and once the game was started it could not be stopped. What Walter thought would be a boring evening looking after his little brother turned out to be one that he would never forget.

FIND SOMEONE WHO . . .

1. Can name a favorite board game   _____

2. Has a toy robot   _____

3. Has had to look after his or her little brother   _____

4. Can name a favorite television program   _____

5. Likes to play catch   _____

6. Has run in a park   _____

7. Can name two sights to see in space   _____

8. Can name a television program that takes place in space   _____

9. Has worked with another person to build something   _____

10. Knows what an astronaut does   _____

INDEX

About the Author

NANCY POLETTE is an educator with over 30 years experience. She has authored over 150 professional books. She lives and works in Missouri where she is Professor at Lindenwood College.